Simply Learn QuickBooks Online

The Complete Illustrated Step-by-Step Guide for Beginners

TeachUcomp, Inc.

The Amazon Endure typeface was designed by 2K/DENMARK in 2025.
Template id: ST-414D415A-25-A01
Printed in The United States.
ISBN: 978-195-8446-41-6
Version 1.3 Revised 1-2026

ABOUT THIS BOOK

Simply Learn QuickBooks Online helps you learn how to use the QuickBooks Online software in a simplified, visually focused way using many pictures and simple step-by-step instructions. All content in this book is derived from our full QuickBooks Online course, titled *Mastering QuickBooks Online Made Easy*™.

CONTENTS

ACKNOWLEDGMENTS

CHAPTER 1 - THE QUICKBOOKS ONLINE ENVIRONMENT

1.1- Learn about QuickBooks Online

QuickBooks Online is an online accounting software program. It helps businesses track their money. It has many features that let its users track sales, purchases, payroll, and more. In addition to tracking money to make financial reporting and accounting easier for businesses, it also provides many tools to help businesses perform tasks like invoicing customers and paying their bills.

QuickBooks Online is a great program to learn. It helps you save time and money by organizing your company's bookkeeping. You can use it from any computer with internet access.

QuickBooks Online Plus has many features. You can create invoices, pay bills, write checks, track inventory, and manage payroll. You can even use some features on a mobile device.

1.2- Learn about QuickBooks Online Versions

QuickBooks Online offers several different versions of its subscriptions. The Simple Start version helps individuals and small businesses track income and expenses for their basic accounting needs and features invoicing and sales tax calculation. The Essentials version includes all the Simple Start tools and then adds some advanced features like entering and paying bills, time tracking, and multi-user support.

A popular version is the Plus version, which includes everything in the Essentials version plus inventory tracking, project tracking, and budgeting. Finally, the Advanced version, which is designed for larger businesses with complex workflows, offers all the features of the Plus version. It also adds advanced reporting, batch transactions, advanced backup options, and it supports more concurrent users than the other versions.

1.3- Navigating in QuickBooks Online

When you open a company file in QuickBooks Online, you see its interface. First, let's examine the names and locations of the tools you use to navigate the QuickBooks Online interface.

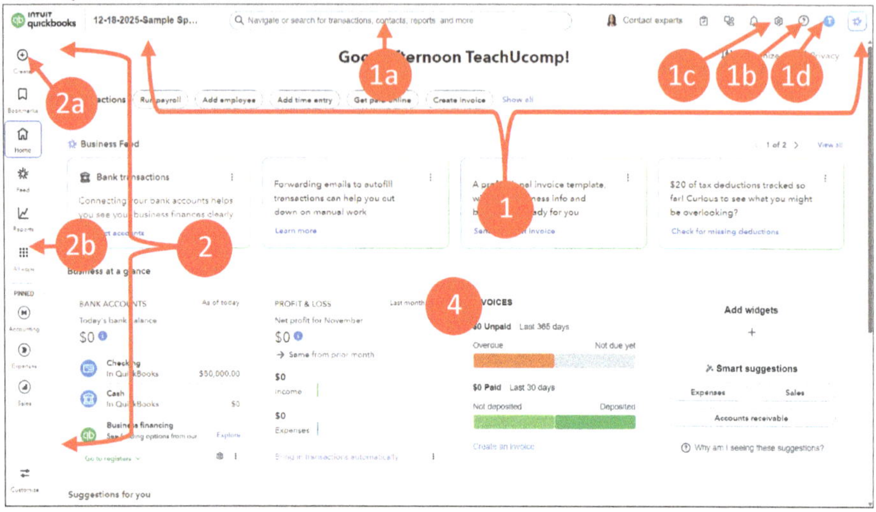

Figure 1: A picture of the QuickBooks Online interface. The numbers and letters match the following objects, except for 3, which appears in the next figure.

1. **The QuickBooks Online toolbar**: This toolbar shows the name of the current company file. It contains buttons you can use on almost every page. These are the most important buttons in this toolbar, which you will use often when using QuickBooks Online:
    a. *The Search field*: You use this to find transactions.
    b. *The Help button*: You can click this to find help in QuickBooks Online.
    c. *The Settings button*: This button looks like a gear icon. You click this button to show a menu of lists and settings. The menu has headings: "Your Company," "Lists," "Tools," and "Profile." The links under each heading let you change information or access tools and features.
    d. *The User button*: You click this button to perform tasks for your Intuit account.

2. **The Navigation Bar**: This bar appears at the left side of the interface. It contains the "+ Create" button, which you use to create new transactions.
    a. *The "+ Create" button*: Hover over this button to show a menu of links you can click to create new transactions.
    b. *The "All apps" button*: Hover over this button to see a listing of "apps," which are like the Navigation Bar categories in the older QuickBooks Online interface. Hover over an app to see its menu of page links. Click a page link to show its page content to the right in the Page Content window. After you click a link, the Apps then appear in a "All apps" bar at the left of the window.
3. **The "All apps" bar**: This bar contains a listing of "apps" you can click to collapse or expand their page links. When expanded, then click a page link to show it in the page content window to the right. To show or hide the "All apps" bar, click the button in its upper-right corner.

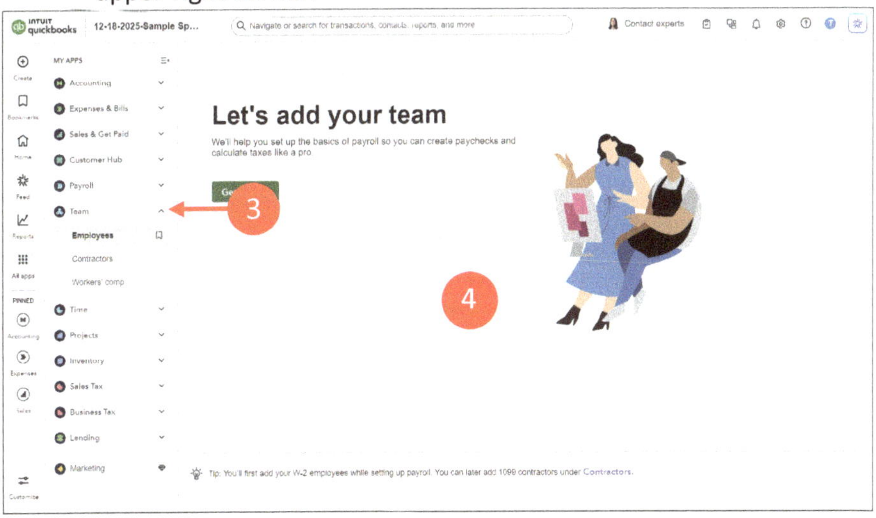

Figure 2: A picture showing the "All apps" bar at the left side of the QuickBooks Online interface. It appears to the right of the Navigation Bar. You can click the button in its upper-right corner to show or hide it.

4. **The Page Content window**: This window appears to the right of the Navigation Bar and "All apps" bar and below the QuickBooks Online toolbar. This window shows the content of the selected page link.

1.4- Learn about Lists and Pages in QuickBooks Online

In QuickBooks Online, you keep important information in lists. These lists include vendors, customers, products, services, and accounts. This way, you don't have to type the same information over and over when you use it in a transaction form. You can add to these lists anytime.

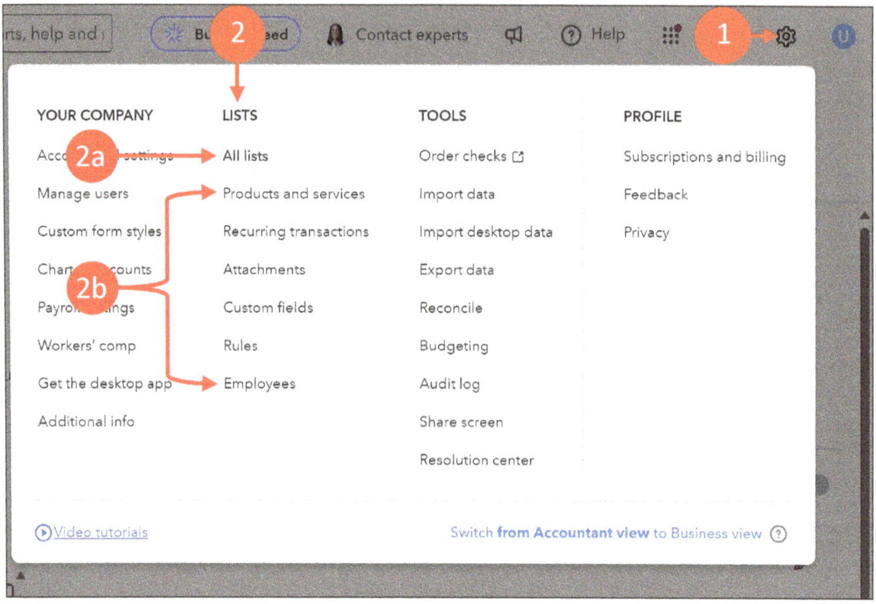

Figure 3: A picture of the menu that appears when you click the "Settings" button in the QuickBooks Online toolbar. The numbers and letters match the following steps.

To see many common lists in QuickBooks Online:

1. Click the "Settings" button.
2. Look under "Lists" to see links to "All lists," "Products and services," "Recurring transactions," "Attachments," "Custom fields," "Rules," and "Employees."
    a. To View More Lists: Click "All lists" to see common lists like "Chart of Accounts," "Products and Services," and "Payment Methods."
        i. Click a list link to open it.
    b. To Directly Access Other Lists: Click other links under "Lists" in the "Settings" menu to go directly to those pages.

QuickBooks Online also keeps many other lists, like customers, vendors, and employees. It also keeps lists of the transactions you create. It shows all these lists within their related pages, which you open using the page links in the "All apps" bar. For example, to view the list of invoices, click the "Sales & Get Paid" app in the "All apps" bar to expand its list of links and then click its “Invoices” link to show the Invoices list in the page content area to the right.

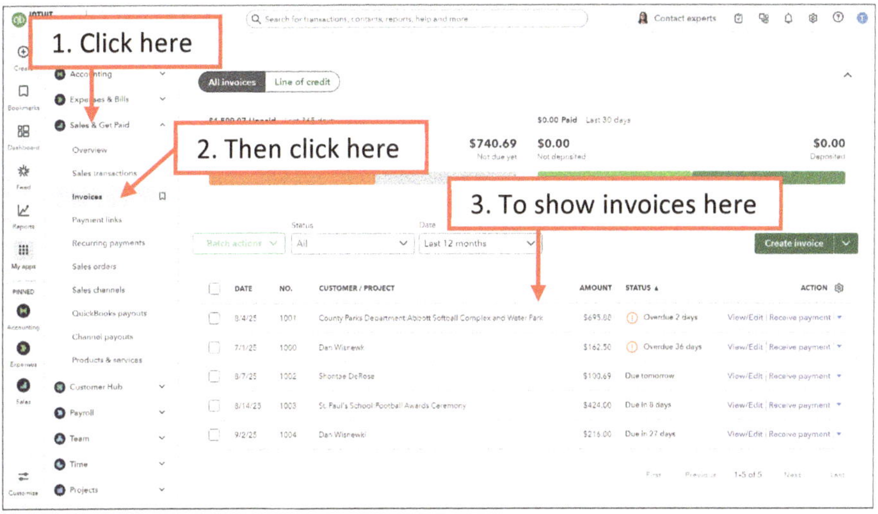

Figure 4: A picture showing how to access the Invoices list in QuickBooks Online.

CHAPTER 2- THE CHART OF ACCOUNTS

2.1- Using the Chart of Accounts in QuickBooks Online

The chart of accounts in QuickBooks Online is a list of all your company's accounts.

To open the chart of accounts in QuickBooks Online:

1. Click the "Settings" button in the QuickBooks Online toolbar.
2. Click "Chart of accounts" under "Your company."

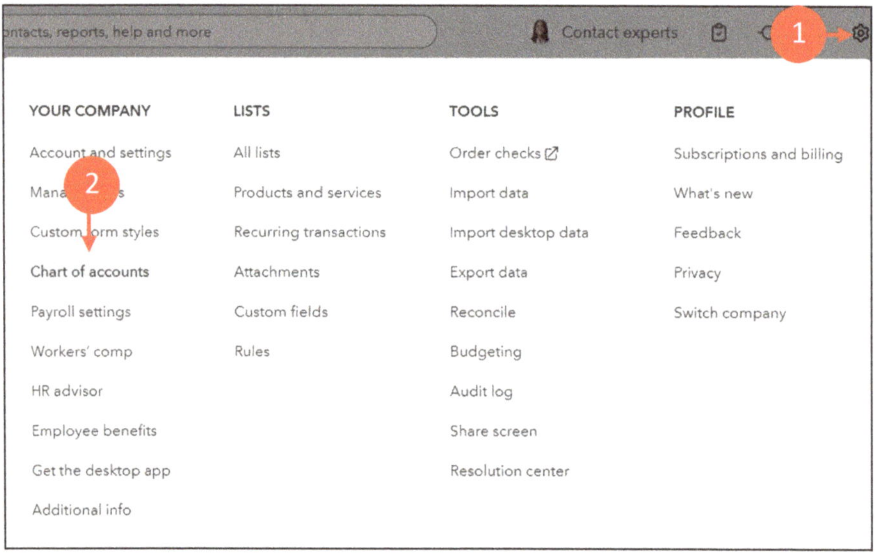

Figure 5: A picture showing how to access the Chart of Accounts in QuickBooks Online. The numbers match the preceding steps.

Accounts are grouped by type: assets, liabilities, equity, income, expenses, other income and expenses, and non-posting accounts. Each account is shown in a row with columns for its name, type, balance, and account actions.

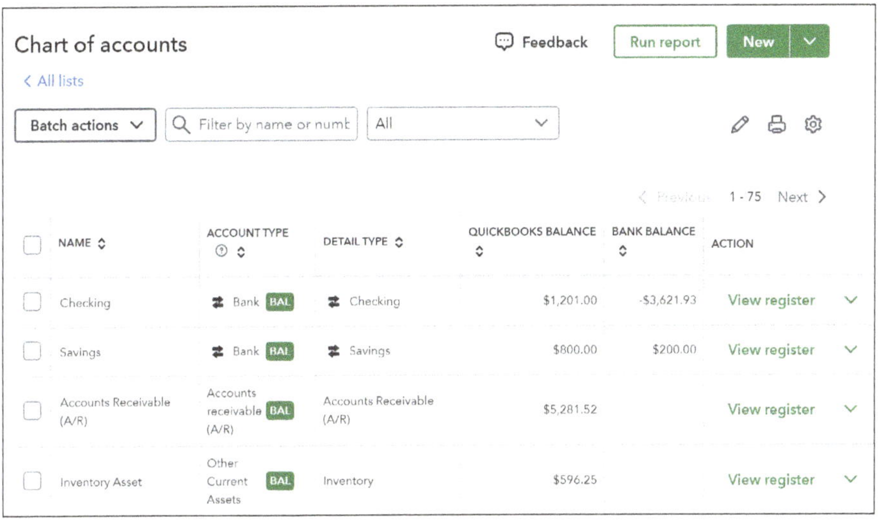

Figure 6: A picture of the Chart of Accounts page in QuickBooks Online.

To find an account, use the "Filter by name or number" field. To show more columns, click the "Settings" gear button above the list and check the boxes for the columns you want.

To view an account register or report:

1. Click "View Register" or "Run Report" in the "Action" column.

To inactivate an account:

1. Click the drop-down arrow in the "Action" column.
2. Select "Make inactive."
3. Confirm in the popup window.

To edit an account:

1. Click the drop-down arrow in the "Action" column.
2. Select "Edit."
3. Edit the account information in the pane on the right.
4. Click "Save" to save changes and close the pane.

At the top of the page, you can run reports, create new accounts, or import accounts. Use the "Batch edit" button to change multiple accounts at once. Click "Print" to get a printer-friendly list.

To change how the chart of accounts looks, click the "Settings" button. You can show or hide columns, include inactive accounts, change the number of accounts per page, and adjust row spacing.

2.2- Adding New Accounts in QuickBooks Online

You can add new accounts in QuickBooks Online anytime. When creating a company, if you add a new balance sheet account (asset, liability, equity), enter its opening balance from the start date. The start date is when you start recording all transactions in QuickBooks Online. This keeps your financial reports accurate. After the start date, you usually don't enter opening balances because you need to record transactions showing where the account gets its funds.

To add new accounts in QuickBooks Online:

1. Click the “Settings” button in the QuickBooks Online toolbar.
2. Click “Chart of accounts” under “Your company.”
3. Click the “New” button in the upper-right corner.

4. In the "New account" pane:

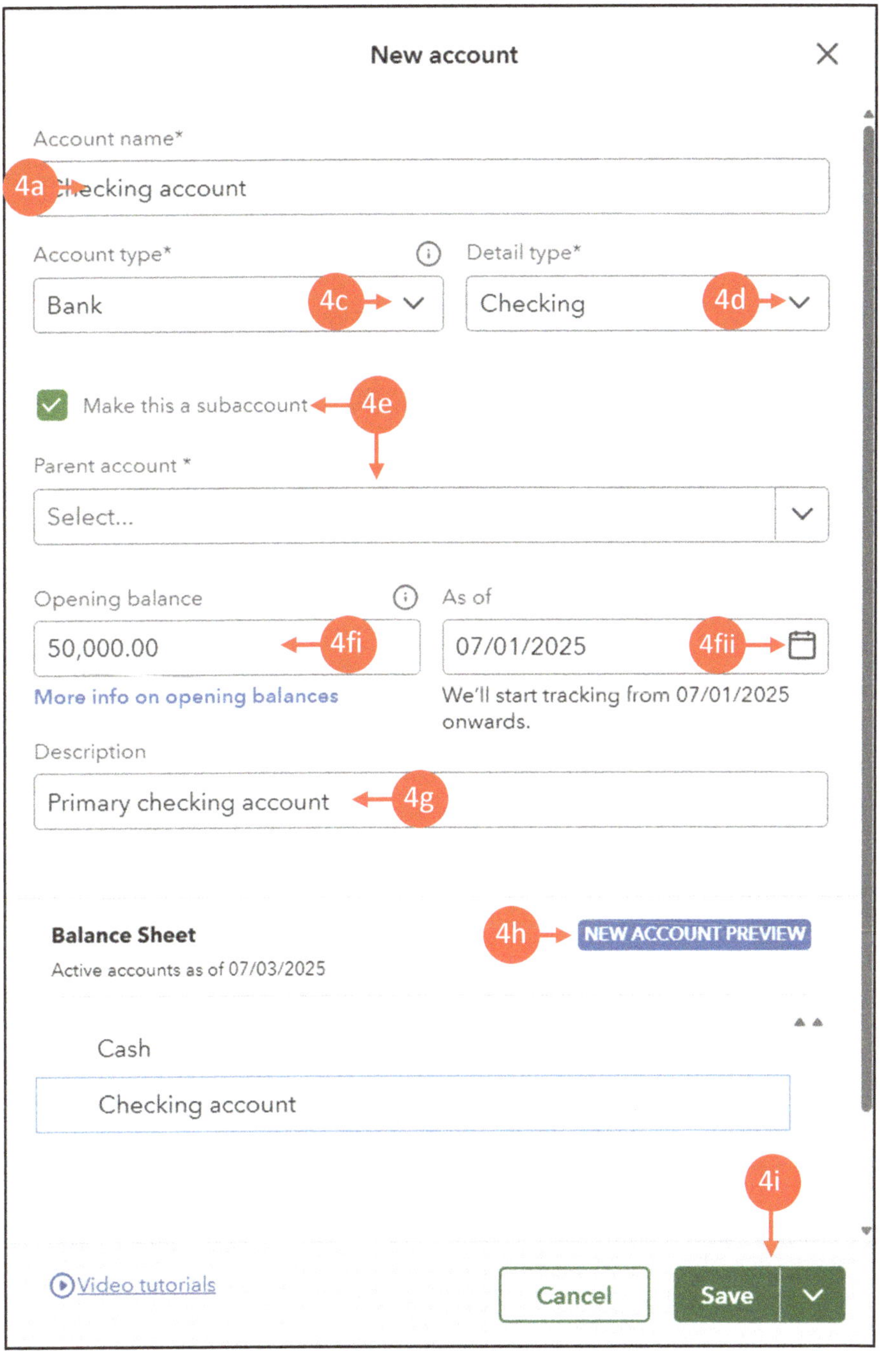

Figure 7: A picture of the "New account" pane in QuickBooks Online. The numbers and letters match the following steps.

a. Enter the account name.
b. If needed, enter an account number.
c. Select the account type from the drop-down menu.
d. Choose the account detail type if needed.
e. If needed, to make it a subaccount, check the box and select its parent account.
f. If needed, to enter opening balances for balance sheet accounts (assets, liabilities, equity):
    i. Enter the opening balance.
    ii. Select the date for the opening balance.
g. Optionally, add a description.
h. The "New Account Preview" shows how the account will look in reports.
i. Click "Save" to finish or "Save and new" to create another account.

2.3- Assigning Account Numbers in QuickBooks Online

QuickBooks Online uses account names to identify accounts. You can also add account numbers and choose to show them in forms and reports. Before assigning account numbers, you must enable them. Account numbers can be up to 20 digits long.

To enable account numbers in QuickBooks Online:

1. Click the "Settings" button in the QuickBooks Online toolbar.
2. Click "Account and settings" under "Your Company."

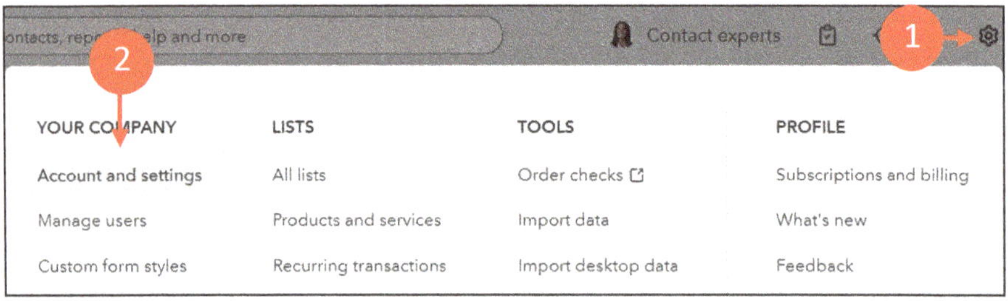

Figure 8: A picture showing the locations of the preceding steps 1 and 2.

3. Click "Advanced" on the left.
4. Click "Chart of Accounts" to edit its settings.
5. Turn on "Enable account numbers."
6. Check "Show account numbers" to see them in forms and reports.

7. Click "Save" and then "Done."

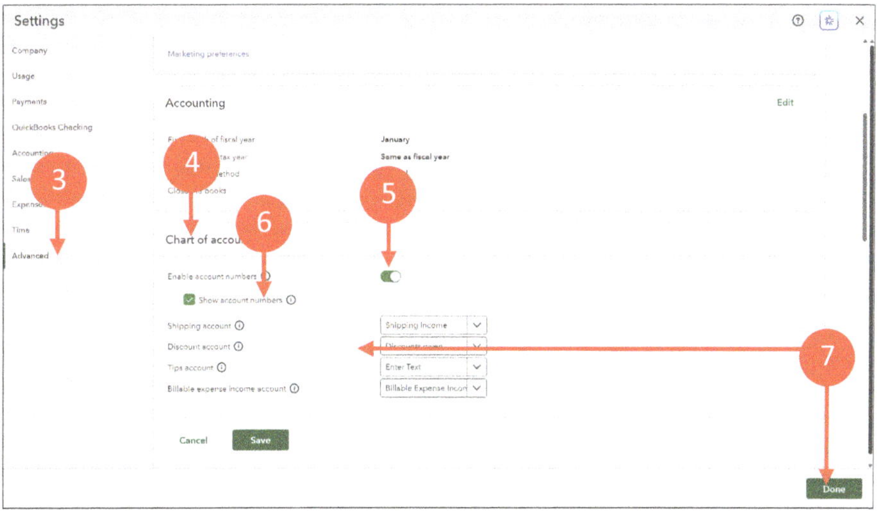

Figure 9: A picture showing the locations of the preceding steps 3 through 7.

To assign account numbers:

1. Click the "Settings" button in the QuickBooks Online toolbar.
2. Click "Chart of accounts" under "Your Company."
3. Click "Batch edit" in the upper-right corner, which looks like a pencil icon.
4. Enter or edit account numbers in the "Number" column.
5. Click "Save" to finish.

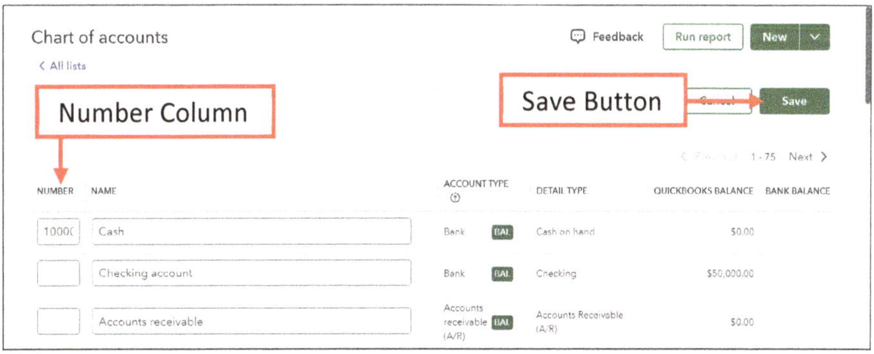

Figure 10: A picture showing the Number column and Save button that appear after you click the Batch edit button in the Chart of Accounts window after enabling account numbers in QuickBooks Online.

CHAPTER 3- CUSTOMERS, EMPLOYEES, AND VENDORS

3.1- Learn about Customers, Employees, and Vendors in QuickBooks Online

QuickBooks Online saves lists of customers, employees, and vendors. This helps you quickly reuse information, so you won't need to retype it each time you use it in a transaction form. Each list appears within its respective page in QuickBooks Online, which you can access from the links under the apps in the "All apps" bar.

To view the Customers list in QuickBooks Online:

1. Click the "Customers" link in the "Customer Hub" app in the "All apps" bar.

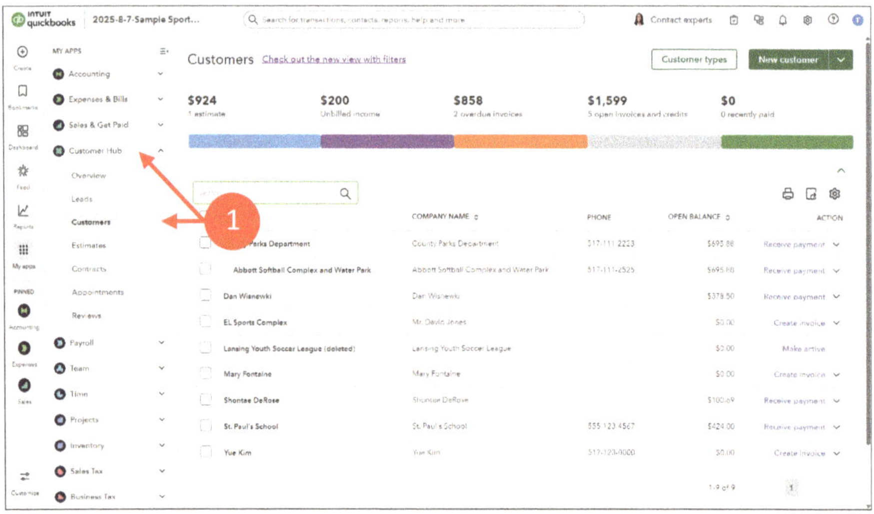

Figure 11: A picture showing how to open the Customers list in QuickBooks Online.

To view the Employees list in QuickBooks Online:

1. Click the "Employees" link in the "Team" app in the "All apps" bar.

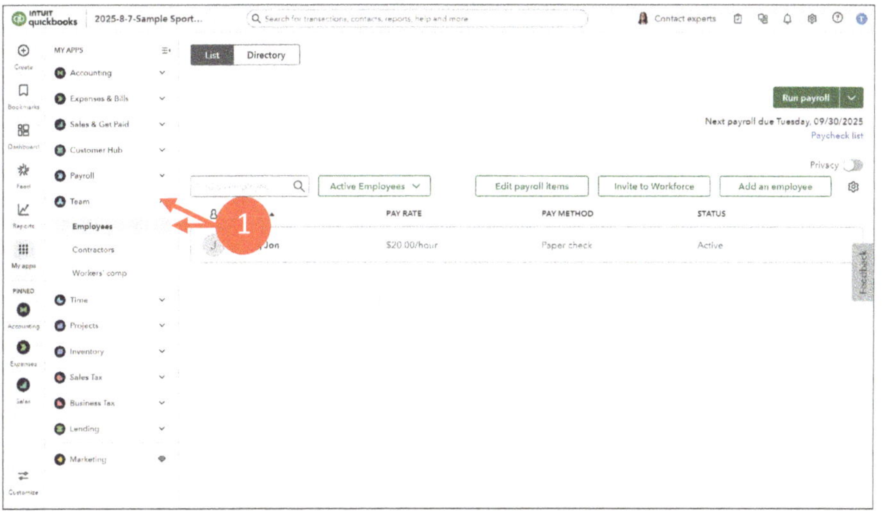

Figure 12: A picture showing how to open the Employees list in QuickBooks Online.

To open the Vendors list in QuickBooks Online:

1. Click the "Vendors" link in the "Expenses & Bills" app in the "All apps" bar.

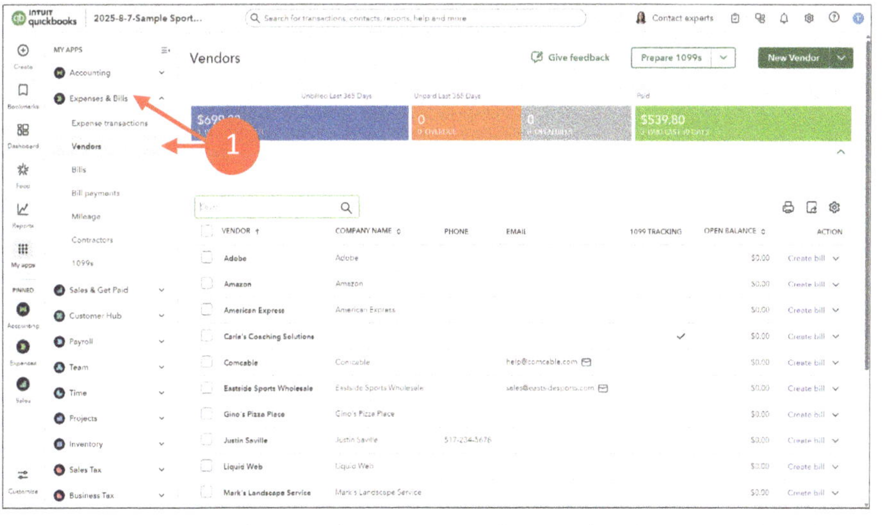

Figure 13: A picture showing how to open the Vendors list in QuickBooks Online.

3.2- Adding a New Customer in QuickBooks Online

In QuickBooks Online, customers are the people and businesses you sell things to, using forms like invoices and sales receipts. Many businesses keep track of each sale to each customer, but others don't. For example, a food truck might sell food for cash and use a cash register. Instead of recording each sale, they might just add up all the cash sales for the day and enter that total in QuickBooks Online. They can create one customer called "Cash Register Sales" to record these daily totals.

To add a new customer:

1. Open the Customers list.
2. Click “Add customer manually” or “New customer” in the upper-right corner.
3. Fill in the customer’s name, contact info, and other details in the “Customer” pane. The “Customer” pane has sections for:

    a. **Name and contact**: Enter the customer’s name, company name, email, phone, and other contact info.

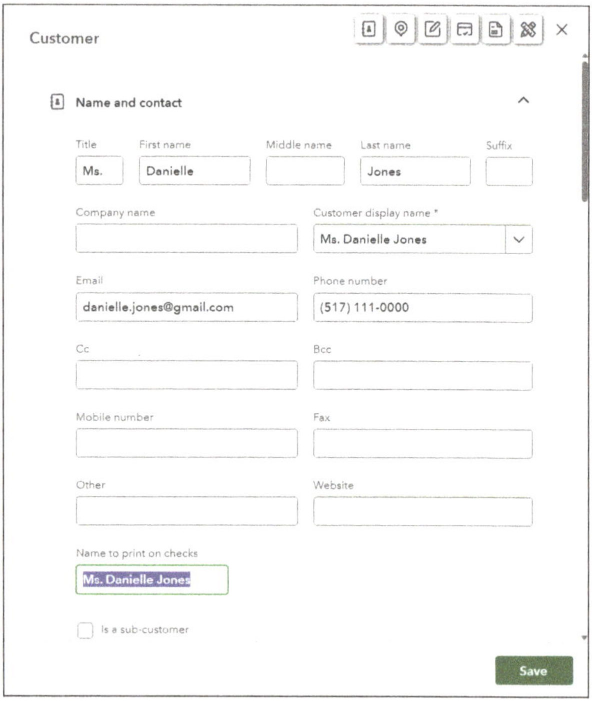

Figure 14: A picture showing the "Name and contact" section within the Customer pane in QuickBooks Online.

b. **Communication permissions**: Lets you select the customer's email address and confirm marketing email permission after entering their email.
c. **Addresses**: Enter billing and shipping addresses.
d. **Notes and attachments**: Add notes and attachments.
e. **Payments**: Set the primary payment method and payment terms.
f. **Additional info**: Set customer type, tax status, credit limit, and default tax rate.

4. Click "Save" to finish.

3.3- Using the Customers Page and Customers List in QuickBooks Online

The Customers page in QuickBooks Online has a Money Bar at the top, followed by a list of your customers. The Money Bar at the top of the page shows customer estimates, billing, and invoicing. Click any section to filter the Customers list below. Click the "Clear filter/View all" link to remove the filter. Click the arrow in its lower-right corner to collapse or expand the Money Bar.

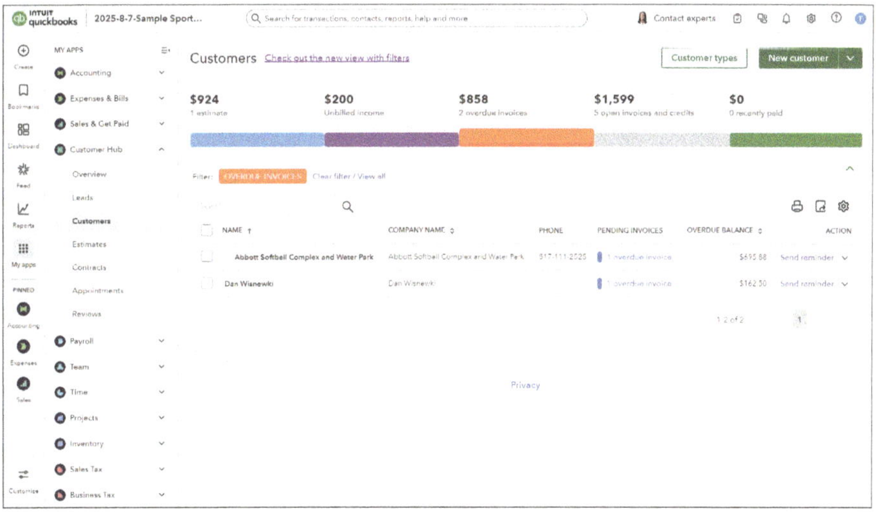

Figure 15: A picture of the Customers page in QuickBooks Online. The Money Bar at the top of the page is filtering the Customers list below it.

The previous lesson showed you how to manually add a new customer in QuickBooks Online. However, you can also import customers or add multiple customers at once, if needed.

To import new customers or add multiple customers at once:

1. To import customers, click the "New customer" button's drop-down arrow and select "Import customers."
2. To add multiple customers, click the "New customer" button's drop-down arrow and select "Multiple customers."

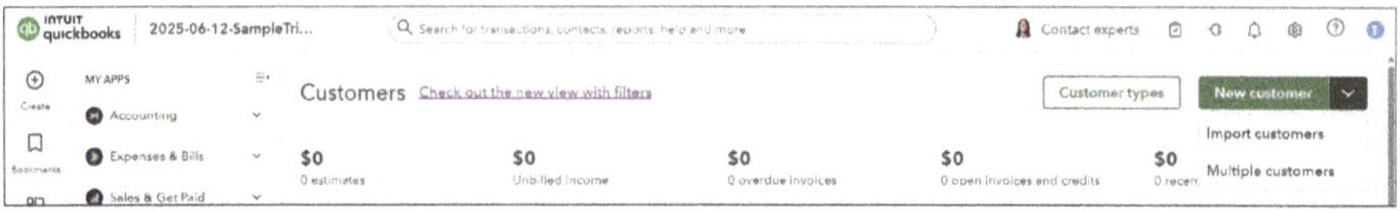

Figure 16: A picture showing the "Import customers" and "Multiple customers" commands that appears when you click the drop-down on the "New customer" button in the Customers page in QuickBooks Online.

Below the Money Bar is the Customers list. The Customers list shows columns of customer information. Each customer appears as a row in the list. You use this list to manage them. You can also perform many "Actions" for selected customers, like making an invoice.

Additionally, there is a "Search" field above the list and three buttons for "Print," "Export to Excel," and "Settings" in its upper-right corner.

To perform batch actions on customers:

1. Check the boxes next to the customers you want to select.
2. Click the "Batch actions" button above the list.
3. Choose what you want to do, like "Create statements," "Email," "Make inactive," or "Select customer type."

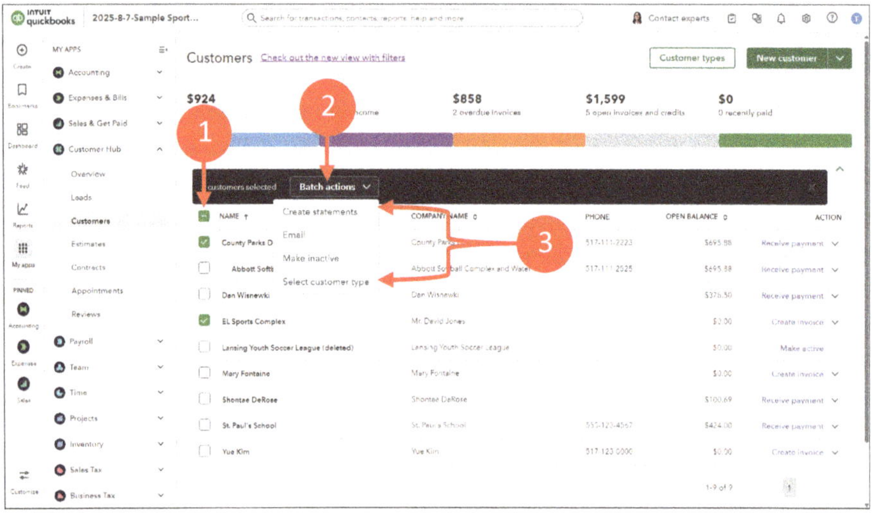

Figure 17: A picture showing how to perform batch actions on customers in the Customers list in QuickBooks Online. The numbers match the preceding activity steps.

To sort the Customers list:

1. Click the sort button in the "Name," "Company Name," "Attachments," or "Open Balance" column heading.
2. Look for the arrow next to the column title:
    a. Upward arrow means the list is sorted from A to Z (ascending).
    b. Downward arrow means the list is sorted from Z to A (descending).
3. To change the sort order, click the arrow again.

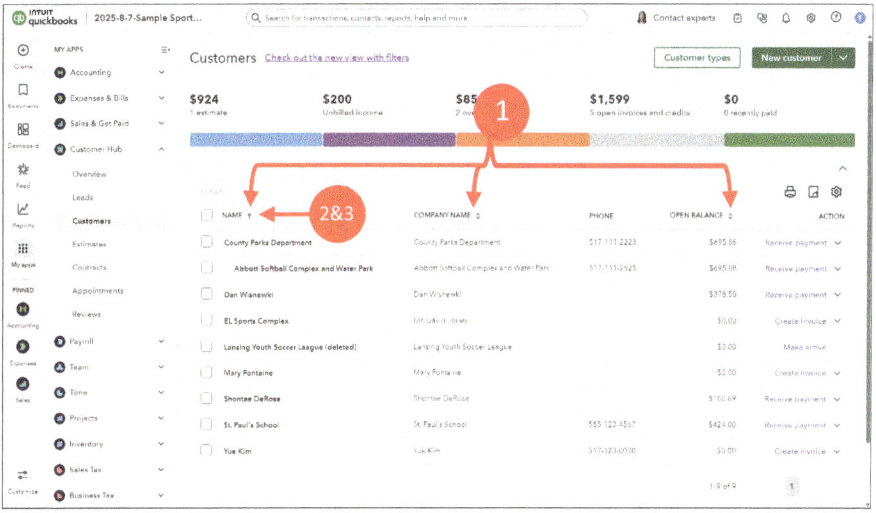

Figure 18: A picture showing the sort buttons and the sort arrow icon you use to sort by columns in the Customers list in QuickBooks Online. The numbers match the preceding steps.

To find a customer in the Customers list:

1. Type a name or company into the "Search" field at the top of the Customers list.
2. Press the "Enter" key on your keyboard.
3. To see all customers again, delete what you typed in the "Search" field.

4. Press the "Enter" key again.

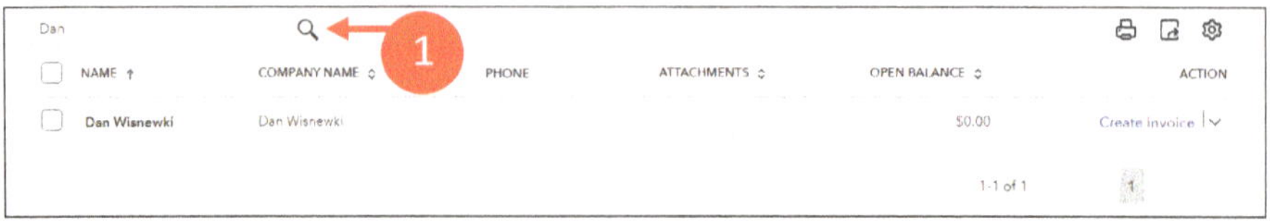

Figure 19: A picture of the "Search" field above the Customers list in QuickBooks Online. The number matches the step in the preceding activity.

To print the Customers list, export it to Excel, or change its display options:

1. To print the Customers list, click the "Print" button.
2. To download the Customers list as an Excel file, click the "Export to Excel" button.
3. To change the display options for the Customers list, click the "Settings" button.

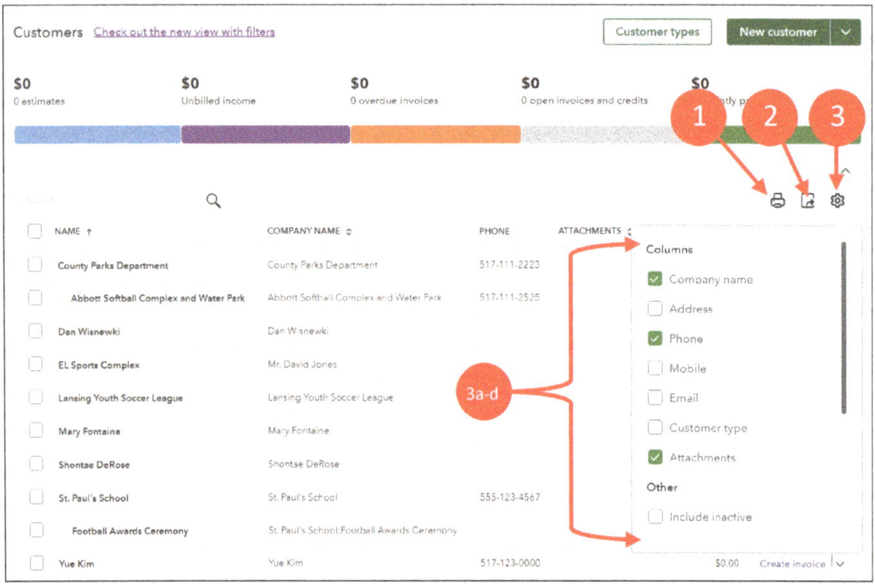

Figure 20: A picture showing how to print the Customers list, export it to Excel, or change its display options. The numbers and letters match the steps in this activity.

   a. To show or hide columns, check or uncheck the column names under "Columns."
   b. To show inactive customers, check the "Include inactive" box under "Other."

c. To show customer projects, check the "Include projects" box.

d. To choose how many rows to show per page, select the number under "Page size."

To perform an action on a customer:

1. Find the customer you want to act on.
2. Click the drop-down in the "Action" column for that customer.
3. Choose an action from the list.
4. Clicking any action (except "Make inactive") opens a window or page to complete the task.

Figure 21: A picture showing some of the possible actions that can appear when you click the drop-down in the "Action" column for a customer in QuickBooks Online.

To move through multiple pages of the Customers list, if needed:

1. Click the left-pointing and right-pointing arrow button icons in the lower-right corner of the Customers list.

To edit customers or view customer transactions:

1. Click the customer's name in the Customers list.
2. On the customer detail page, click the tabs to show the related customer information.
3. To edit the customer's information, click the "Edit" button at the top right.
   a. Change the information in the pane that opens.
   b. Click the "Save" button at the bottom of the pane.
4. To see transactions for the customer:
   a. Click the "Transaction List" tab.

   b. Click a transaction to see more details and edit it if needed.

5. To return to the Customers list, click the “< Customers” link in the upper-left.

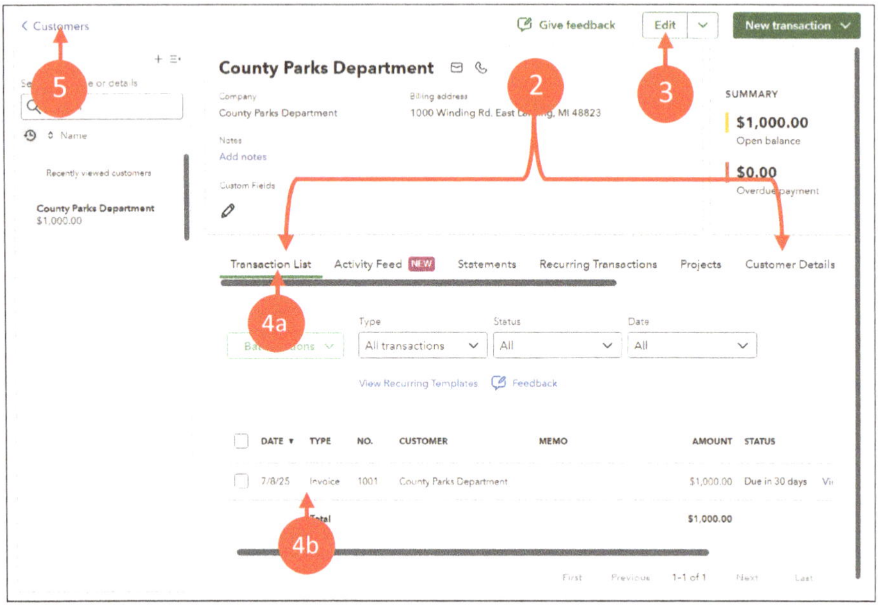

Figure 22: A picture of a customer's details page in QuickBooks Online. The numbers and letters correspond to the steps and objects in the preceding activity.

You can't delete a customer in QuickBooks Online, but you can make them inactive. This hides them in the Customers list. It's best to only make customers inactive if they don't owe any money (no "open balance" amount) to avoid making an adjusting entry to fix their open balance.

To inactivate a customer:

1. *From the customer detail page*: Click the drop-down on the "Edit" button in the top right and select "Make inactive."

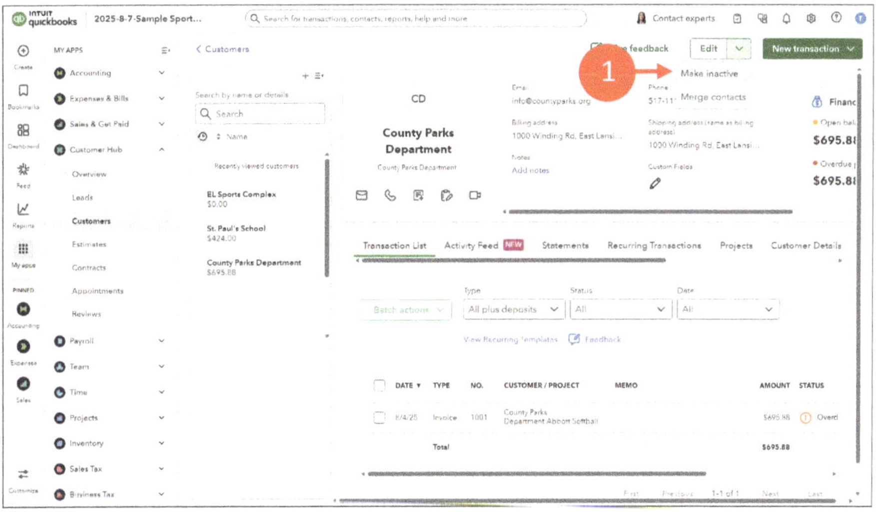

Figure 23: The "Make inactive" command in the customer's details page.

2. *From the Customers list*: Select the "Make inactive" choice from the "Action" column for the customer.

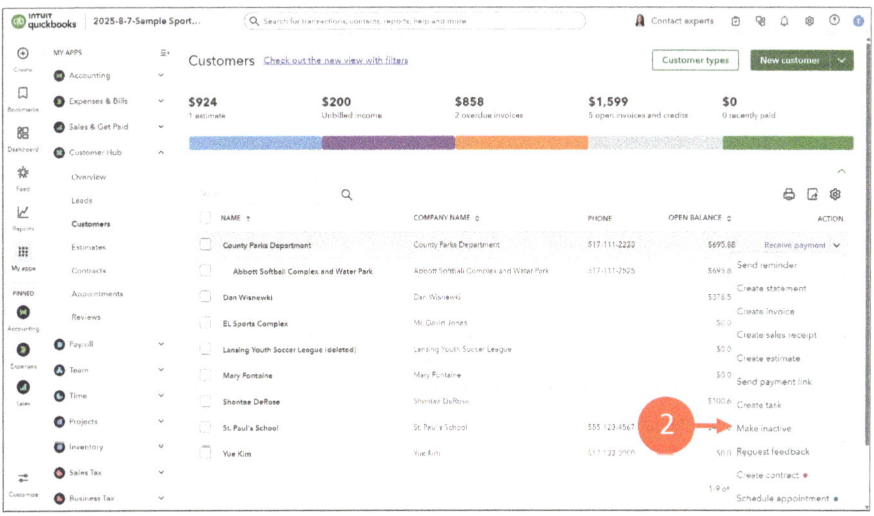

Figure 24: The "Make inactive" command in the Customers list.

3. If the customer has no open balance:
    a. A window opens, asking you to confirm.
        i. To confirm, click "Yes, make inactive."

Figure 25: A picture of the customer inactivation confirmation window if the customer has no open balance in QuickBooks Online.

4. Alternatively, if the customer has an open balance:
    a. A warning window opens, asking if it's okay to create an adjusting transaction.
        i. To confirm and create the transaction, click "Yes, make inactive."

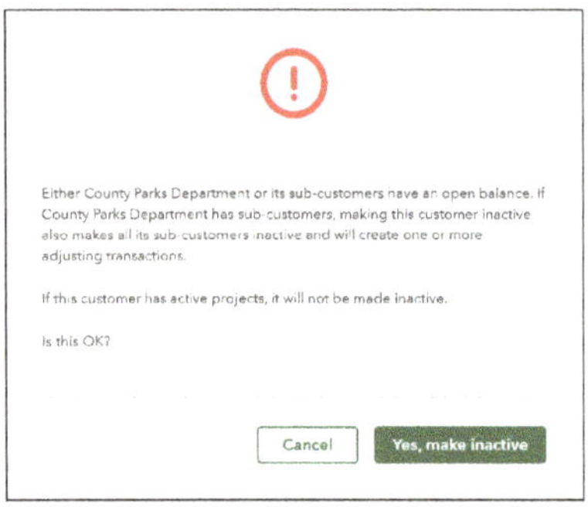

Figure 26: A picture of the inactivation warning window if the customer has an open balance in QuickBooks Online.

Inactive customers do not appear in the Customers list, by default. Before you reactivate an inactive customer, you must first show the inactive customers.

To reactivate an inactive customer in the Customers list:

1. Click the "Settings" button above the Customers list.
2. Check the "Include inactive" box to show the inactive customers.

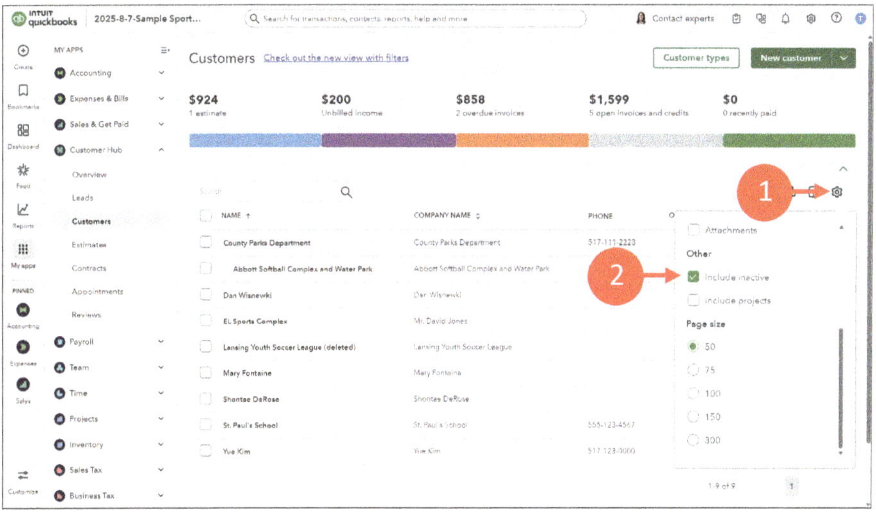

Figure 27: A picture showing how to show inactive customers in QuickBooks Online. The numbers match the steps in this activity.

3. To reactivate a customer, click the "Make active" link in the "Action" column for that customer.

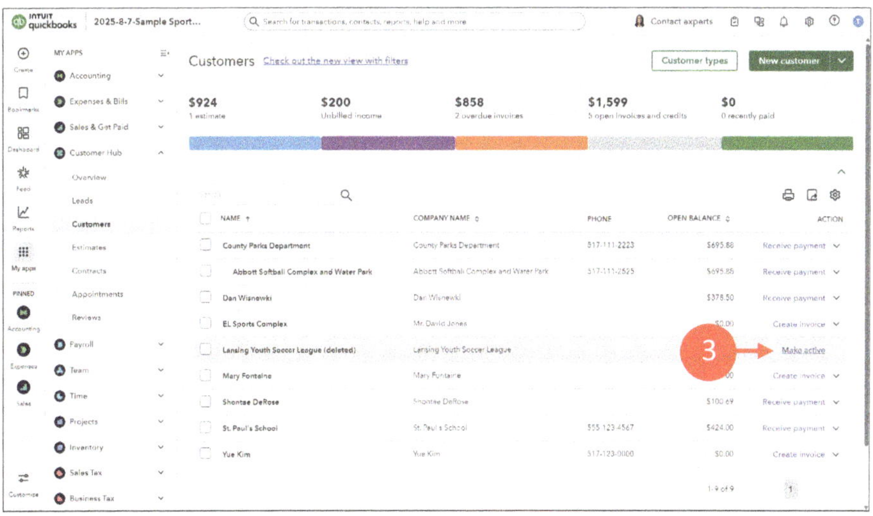

Figure 28: A picture showing how to reactivate an inactive customer in QuickBooks Online. The number matches the step in this activity.

3.4- Adding a New Employee in QuickBooks Online

Employees in QuickBooks Online are the people who work for you. Small business owners can also be employees. Employees get a W-2 form for their earnings. Subcontractors and people who get a 1099 form are not employees; they are entered as vendors. QuickBooks Online keeps employee records in the Employees list in the "Employees" page.

To enter employees into QuickBooks Online:

1. To open the "Employees" page to view the Employees list:
    a. Select either "Team" or "Payroll" in the "All apps" bar.
    b. Then click the "Employees" link.

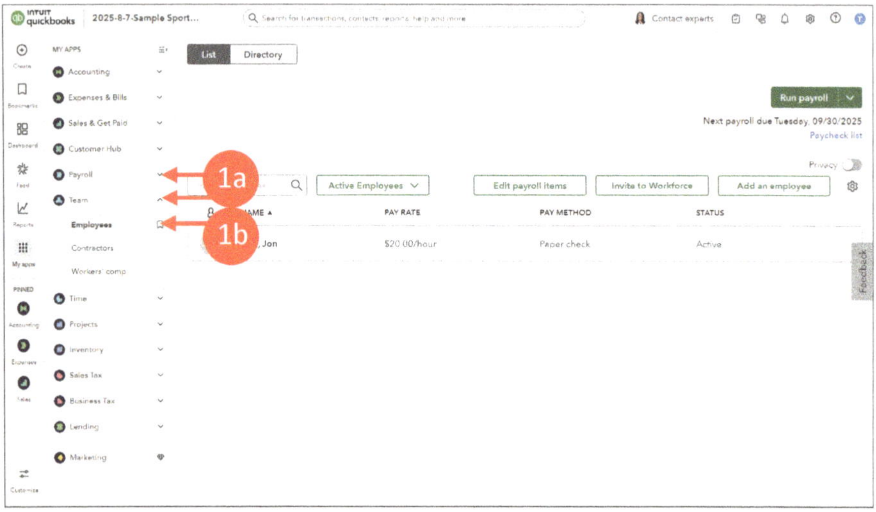

Figure 29: A picture showing how to open the "Employees" page to view the Employees list in QuickBooks Online. The numbers and letters match the steps in this activity.

2. To then add employees if you haven't set up payroll yet and have a QuickBooks payroll subscription:
    a. Click the "Get started" button in the "Employees" page to go to the "Overview" page.
    b. Then click the "Get started" button in the "Overview" page to set up payroll and add the employees during the payroll setup.
3. Alternatively, to add employees for time tracking without a QuickBooks payroll plan:
    a. Click the "Add an employee" button in the "Employees" page.

b. Then enter the employee's information in the employee information window that opens and click "Add employee."

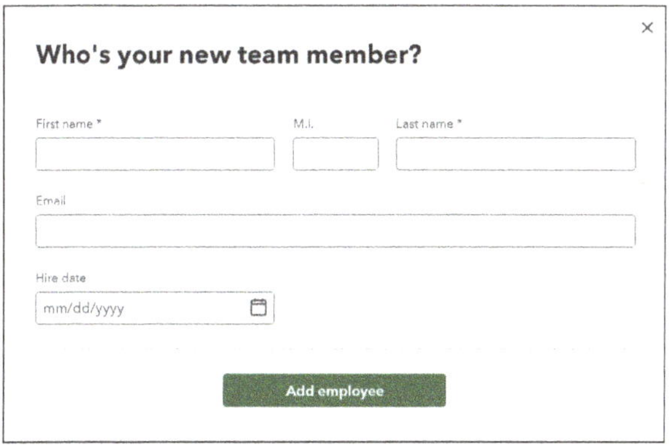

Figure 30: A picture of the employee information window, as shown above in step 3b.

To create a new employee and/or invite the employee to enter their own payroll information into QuickBooks Workforce **after** setting up payroll:

1. Go to the "Employees" page again and click "Add an employee."

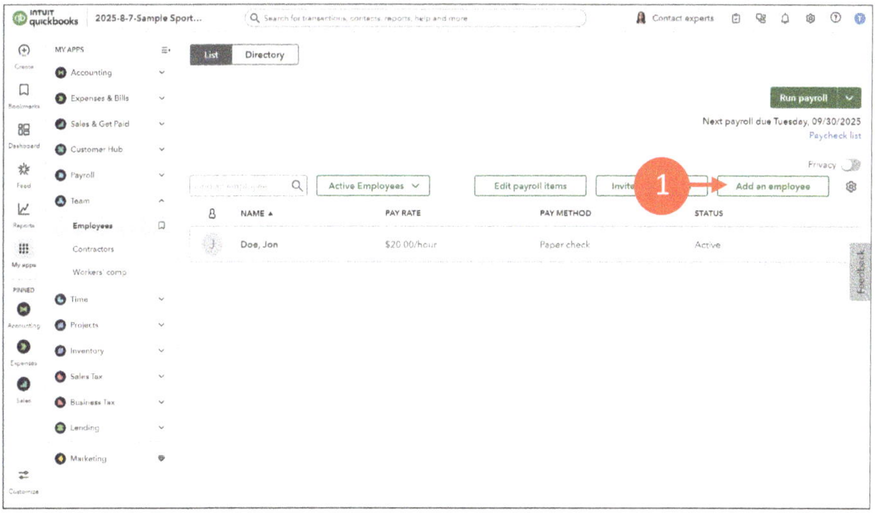

Figure 31: A picture showing how to add an employee after setting up payroll in QuickBooks Online. The number matches the step in this activity.

2. In the window that opens, enter their name, email, and hire date.
3. To choose how to enter the employee's onboarding information, select the desired onboarding option in the "Onboarding" section.
4. To let the employee clock in and out using QuickBooks Workforce, check the "Time tracking" checkbox.

5. Then click "Add employee" to send an invite and/or create the employee.

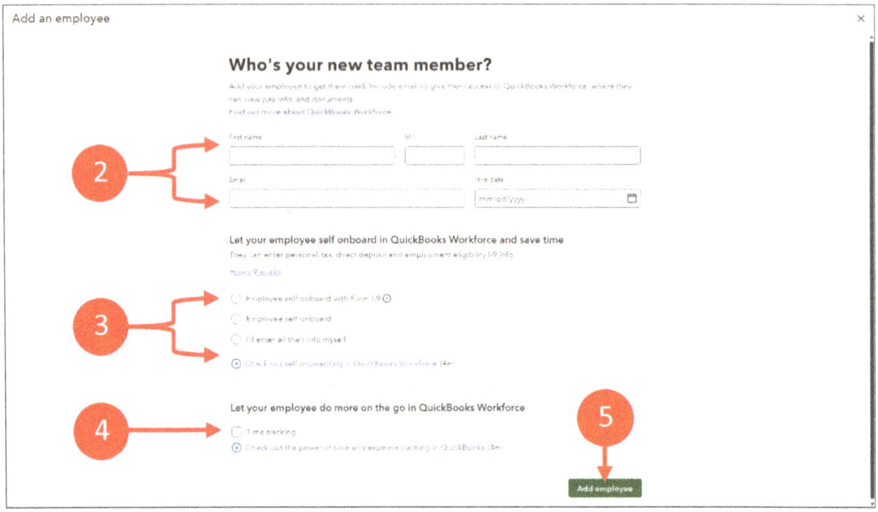

Figure 32: A picture of the "Add an employee" window in QuickBooks Online. The numbers correspond to the steps in this activity.

6. If you chose to enter the employee's onboarding info yourself:
    a. Click the "Finish Payroll Info" button.
    b. Enter their employee information within the sections on the employee's details page within the "Profile" tab.

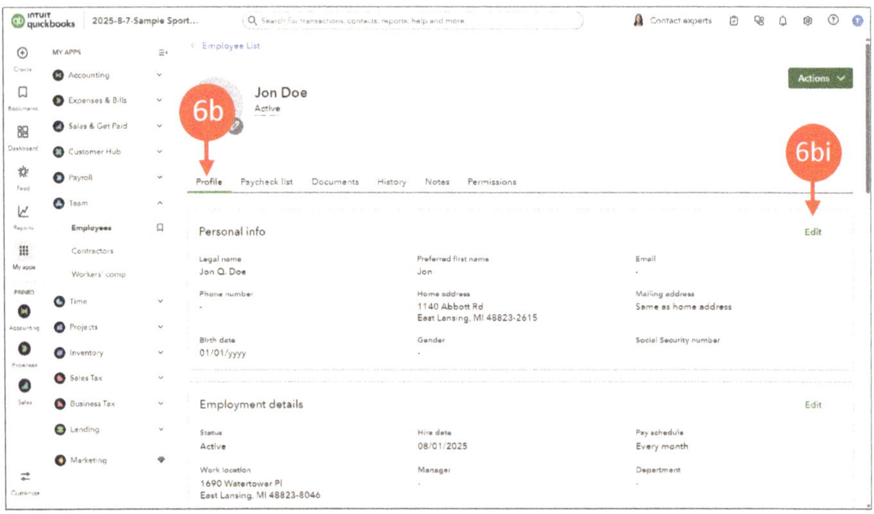

Figure 33: A picture showing the "Profile" tab within the employee's details page. The numbers and letters match the steps in this activity.

i. To enter personal info, click "Edit" in the "Personal info" section.
   1) Then enter all their personal details, like name, address, and social security number.
   2) Click the "Save" button at the bottom of the window to save it.

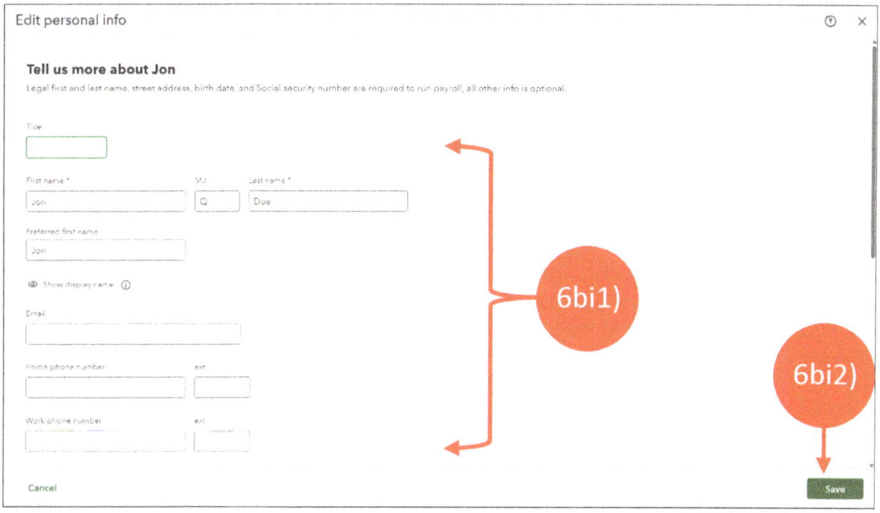

Figure 34: A picture of the fields at the top of the "Edit personal info" window. The numbers and letters match the steps in this activity.

ii. To enter employment details, click "Edit" in the "Employment details" section.
   1) Then select their status, hire date, pay schedule, work location, and enter all the other employment details.
   2) Click the "Save" button at the bottom of the window to save it.

iii. To enter the employee's tax withholdings, click "Edit" in the "Tax withholdings" section.
   1) Then enter all their tax withholding details.
   2) Click the "Save" button at the bottom of the window to save it.

iv. To enter the employee's payment method, click the "Start" or "Edit" link in the "Payment method" section.

1) Then select how to pay the employee and enter all their direct deposit details if needed.
2) Click the "Save" button at the bottom of the window to save it.

v. To enter the employee's base pay, click the "Start" or "Edit" link in the "Base pay" section.

1) Then select the employee's type of base pay and enter their pay rate.
2) Click the "Save" button at the bottom of the pane to save it.

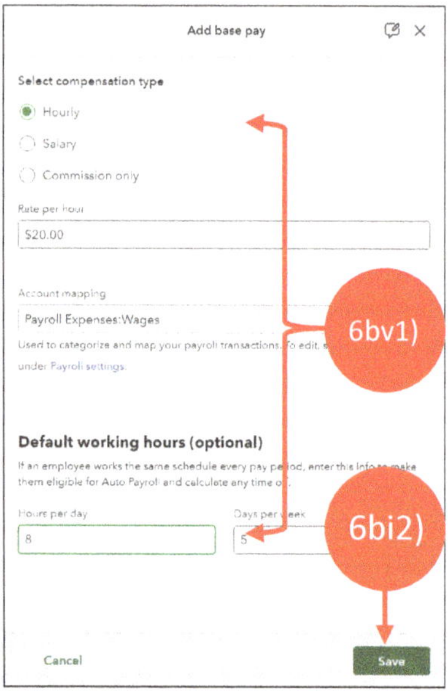

Figure 35: A picture of the "Add base pay" pane in QuickBooks Online. The numbers and letters match the steps in this activity.

vi. To enter any additional pay types, click the "+ Add" link in the "Additional pay types" section.

1) Then select the employee's additional pay types and enter any additional pay info.

2) Click the "Save" button at the bottom of the pane to save it.

vii. To enter the employee's time off, click the "Start" or "Edit" link in the "Time off" section.

1) Then select choices for the different types of time off.
2) Click the "Save" button at the bottom of the window to save it.

viii. To enter the employee's deductions and/or contributions, click the "Start" or "Edit" link in the "Deductions and contributions" section.

1) To set up a deduction or contribution, click "+ Add deduction/contribution," enter its details, and click "Save" in the pane that opens.
2) To set up a garnishment, click "+ Add garnishment," enter its details, and click "Save" in the pane that opens.
3) To edit the details of a deduction, contribution, or garnishment for this specific employee, click its "pencil" icon, make changes, and click "Save" in the pane that opens.
4) When finished, click the "Done" button at the bottom of the window to leave.

ix. To enter emergency contact info for the employee, click the "Start" or "Edit" link in the "Emergency contact" section.

1) Then enter the employee's emergency contact information.
2) Click the "Save" button at the bottom of the window to save it.

c. To view the employee's paycheck list, upload documents like a scanned copy of a paper I-9 form, view employee data changes, enter notes, or set permissions for QuickBooks Workforce, click the "Paycheck list,"

"Documents," "History," "Notes," or "Permissions" tabs within the employee's details page.

d. To return to the Employees list from an employee's details page, click the "< Employee List" link in the upper-left corner.

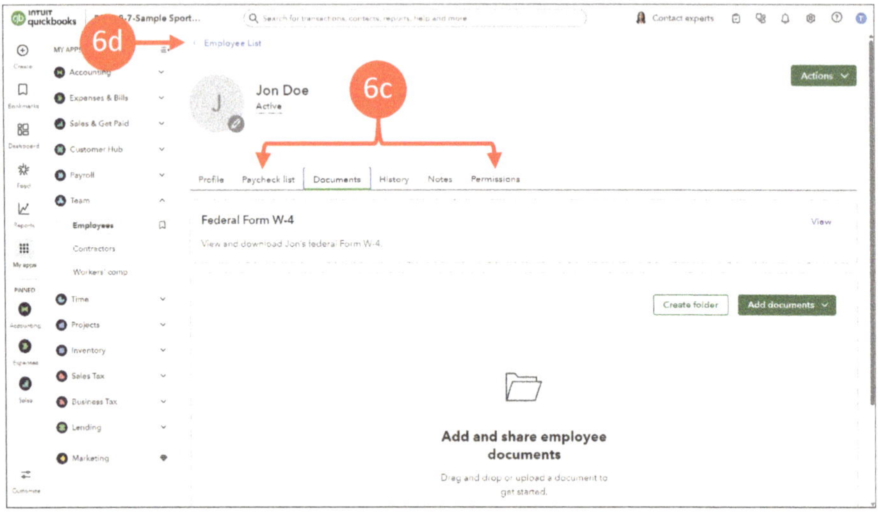

Figure 36: A picture of the other tabs within the employee details page and the link to return to the Employees list. The letters and numbers match the steps in the preceding activity.

3.5- Using the Employees Page and Employees List in QuickBooks Online

QuickBooks Online keeps employee records in the Employees list in the "Employees" page. If you subscribe to a QuickBooks Payroll service, you can set up payroll, enter the employees, and run payroll in QuickBooks Online. If you don't subscribe to a QuickBooks Payroll service, you can still enter employees for time tracking and customer billing, if needed. We saw how to open the "Employees" page to view the Employees list in the previous lesson.

If using QuickBooks Payroll, then after adding employees and running payroll, you'll see a graph of your annual payroll cost appear at the top of the "Employees" page. You can expand or collapse this section by clicking the arrow in its lower-right corner. Below the payroll graph is the Employees list.

To use the "Employees" page and Employees list:

1. To find an employee:
    a. Type their name into the "Find an employee" field, which filters the list as you type.
    b. To show all employees again, delete your entry from this field.

2. To filter the Employees list:
    a. Select a choice from the drop-down to the right of the "Find an employee" field to show active, inactive, or all employees.
3. To sort the Employees list:
    a. Click any column heading to sort by its data.
    b. Each time you click the same column heading, it switches the sort order from ascending to descending order.
4. To edit payroll items if using QuickBooks Payroll:
    a. Click "Edit payroll items."
    b. In the page that opens, click to expand or collapse the payroll item groups.
    c. Click a payroll item in an expanded group to make changes and then save your changes.
    d. Click "Done" to close the page.
5. To invite or remind employees to use QuickBooks Workforce:
    a. Click "Invite to Workforce."
    b. Enter their emails and click the adjacent "Send invite/Send reminder" link to send the invite or reminder.
6. To edit or delete an employee before running a payroll:
    a. Click their name in the Employees list to open their employee details page.
    b. To edit, change their information and save.
    c. To delete, click the "Actions" button, select "Delete employee," and confirm the deletion.

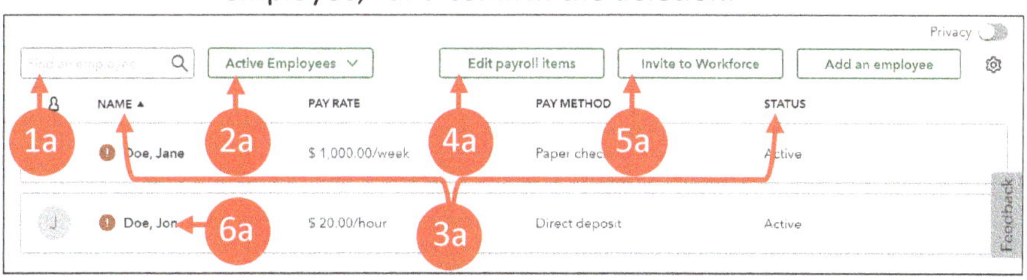

Figure 37: A figure showing the buttons in the "Employees" page, which appear above the Employees list in QuickBooks Online. The numbers and letters match the steps in the preceding activity.

3.6- Adding a New Vendor in QuickBooks Online

The Vendors list within the "Vendors" page tends to be one of the most used and largest lists in QuickBooks Online. You enter any vendor you pay for inventory, products, or services you receive into this list. You also enter subcontractors into this list.

To open the Vendors page in QuickBooks Online:

1. Select “Expenses & Bills” in the "All apps" bar.
2. Then click the “Vendors” link.

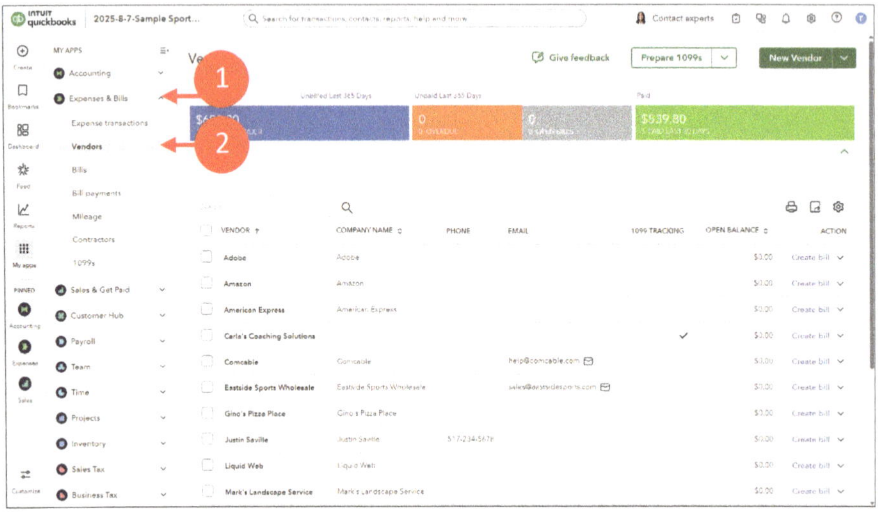

Figure 38: A picture showing how to open the Vendors list in QuickBooks Online. The numbers match the steps in the preceding activity.

To manually add a new vendor:

1. Click “Add vendor” in the middle of the "Vendors" page (first time) or “New vendor” in the upper-right corner of the "Vendors" page.
2. Fill in the vendor’s name, contact info, and other details in the “Vendor” pane. The “Vendor” pane has sections for:

    a. **Name and contact**: Enter the vendor’s company name, email, phone, and other contact info.

    b. **Address**: Enter the vendor’s address.

    c. **Notes and attachments**: Add notes and attachments.

    d. **Bill Pay ACH Info**: Enter bank account and routing numbers for bill payments.

e. **Additional info**: Enter business ID or social security number, track 1099 payments, set cost and billing rates, payment terms, and default expense account.

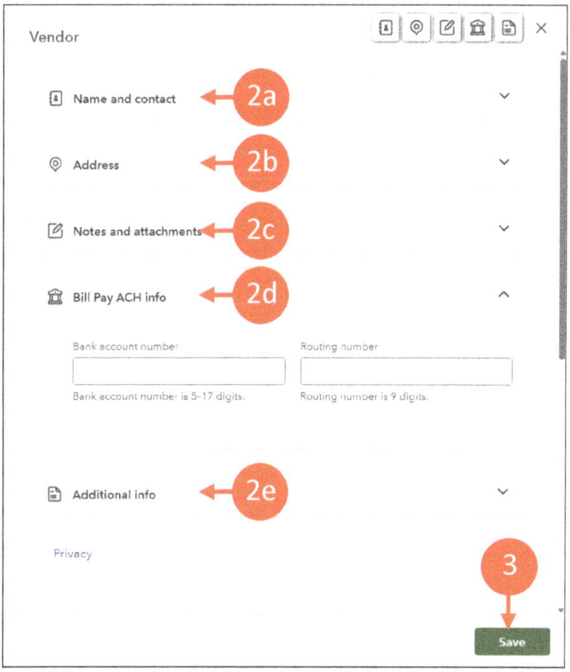

Figure 39: A picture of the sections within the "Vendor" pane. You can click each section to collapse and expand it to show its fields. The numbers and letters match the steps in this activity.

3. Click “Save” to finish.

3.7- Using the Vendors Page and Vendors List in QuickBooks Online

The "Vendors" page in QuickBooks Online has a list of your vendors. You use this list to manage them. You can also perform many “Actions” for selected vendors, like entering a bill.

After adding vendors, you'll see a Money Bar showing vendor transactions at the top of the "Vendors" page. Click any section in the Money Bar to filter the Vendors list. Then click the “Clear Filter/View All” link to remove the filter. Click the arrow in the lower-right corner of the Money Bar to collapse or expand it. Below the Money Bar is the Vendors list.

To use the "Vendors" page and Vendors list:

1. To perform batch actions:
   a. Check the boxes next to the desired vendor names.

   b. Click the “Batch actions” button that then appears above the Vendors list and select a batch action.
2. To use the “Search” field to find a vendor:
   a. Click into the field, type the text by which to filter the list, and press "Enter" on your keyboard.
   b. To show all entries again, delete the typed text and press the "Enter" key on your keyboard.
3. To sort the Vendors list, click its column headings.
4. To print the list, export the list to Excel, or change its display options:
   a. To print the list, click the "Print" button in its upper-right corner.
   b. To export the list to Excel, click the "Export to Excel" button in its upper-right corner.
   c. To change the list's display options, click the “Settings” button in its upper-right corner.
      i. Then check the checkboxes and select options in the drop-down menu that appears to select the columns to show, show inactive vendors, and set the number of vendors to show per page.
5. To create bills, make payments, schedule payments, create expenses, write checks, create purchase orders, or make vendors inactive, click or select a choice from the "Action" column's choice for the desired vendor.

6. To edit a vendor's details, click the vendor's name in the Vendors list.

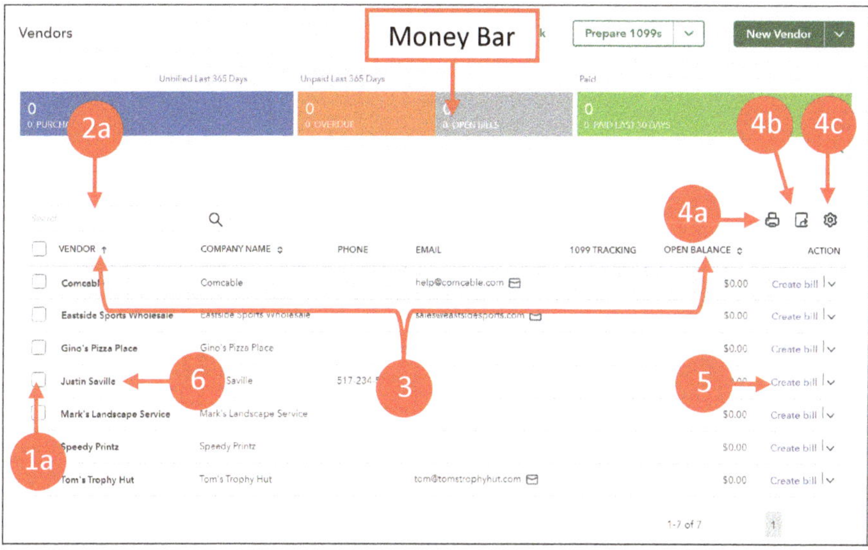

Figure 40: A picture of the Vendors list in the "Vendors" page. It shows the Money Bar, the Vendors list, and buttons in the "Vendors" page. The numbers and letters match the steps in the preceding activity.

To inactivate a vendor, click the "Make inactive" choice in the vendor's "Action" column or select it from the "Edit" button's drop-down menu in the upper-right corner of the vendor's detail page. Then confirm the action if needed. To reactivate an inactive vendor, check the "Include inactive" box in the "Settings" drop-down menu and then click the "Make active" command that appears for the vendor's record in its "Action" column.

CHAPTER 4- MANAGING LIST ITEMS

4.1- Sorting Lists in QuickBooks Online

To sort lists in QuickBooks Online:

1. Click the sort button next to the column heading or click the column heading itself.
2. In newer lists like Customers or Vendors, click the sort button.

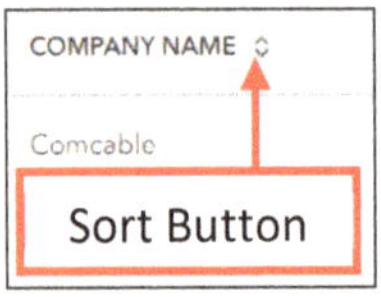

3. In older lists, click the column heading.

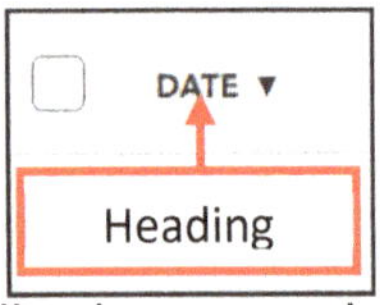

Not all columns can be sorted. To check, look for a sort button or hover over the column heading. If the pointer turns into a hand, you can sort by that column.

Click once to sort in ascending order (A to Z or 1 to 9). Click again to sort in descending order (Z to A or 9 to 1).

4.2- How to Inactivate and Reactivate List Items in QuickBooks Online

Inactivating list items in QuickBooks Online hides them but keeps their information. You can reactivate them later. Only inactivate items with a zero balance. If an item has a balance, QuickBooks makes an adjusting entry. It's better to assign transactions to the correct item first.

To inactivate an item:

1. Open the item's list page and then find the item in the list.
2. Select the “Make inactive” choice from its “Action” column.
3. Confirm the action.

To reactivate an item, except in the Products and services list:

1. Click the “Settings” button in the list's upper-right corner.
2. Check the “Include inactive” checkbox to show inactive items.

3. Click the "Make active" link in the item's "Action" column.

To reactivate an item in the Products and services list:

1. Click the "Filter" drop-down button at the top of the list, select "Inactive" from the "Status" drop-down, and click "Apply."
2. Click "Make active" in the "Action" column for the item to reactivate and then confirm it in the window that opens.
3. Click the "Clear filters" link above the list to show all active items again.

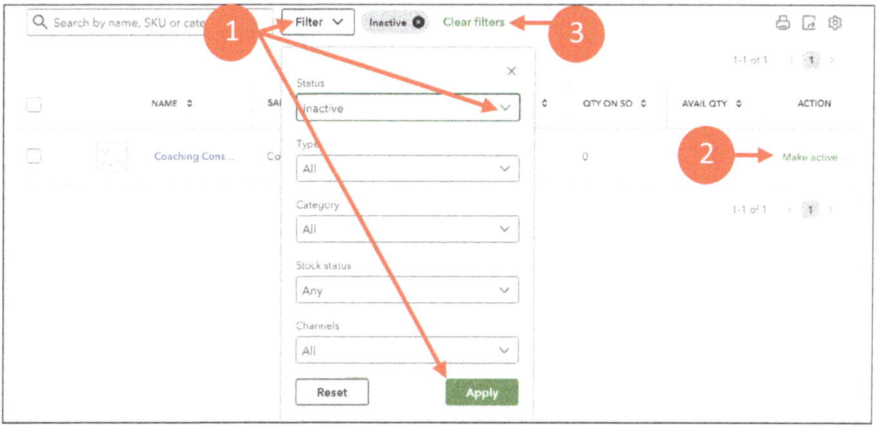

Figure 41: A picture showing how to reactivate an item in the Products and services list. The numbers match the steps in the preceding activity.

4.3- How to Rename and Merge List Items in QuickBooks Online

In QuickBooks Online, you can rename or merge items in a list. Merging helps fix mistakes when multiple people enter data.

For example, if you have "Mowing" and "Lawn Mowing" services, you can merge them into one.

To rename an item:

1. Open the item's editing pane.
2. Change the item's name.
3. Save the changes.

To merge items:

1. Open the editing pane of the item to merge.
2. Change the name to match the item you want to keep.
3. Save the changes.

4. Confirm the merge when prompted.

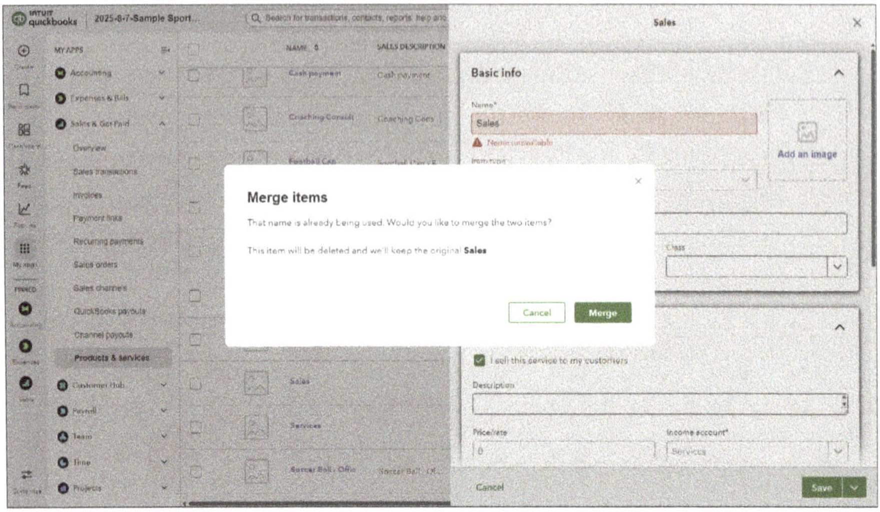

Figure 42: A picture showing a user merging two items within the Products and services list into one.

To merge customer or vendor contacts in their lists:

1. Click the contact's name to merge transactions from in its list to show its details page.
2. Click the drop-down arrow on the contact's "Edit" button and select "Merge contacts."

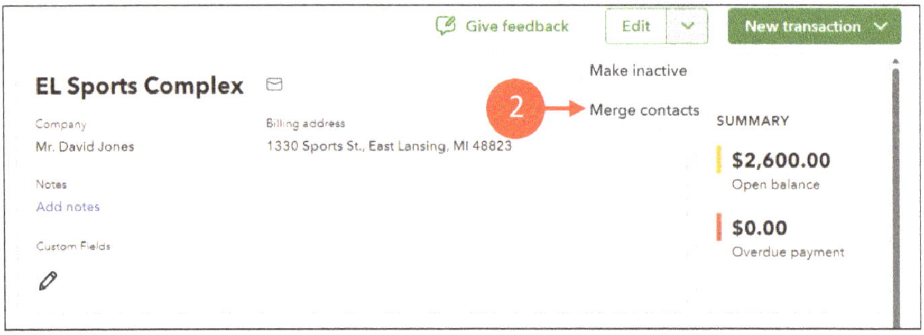

Figure 43: A picture showing the location of the "Merge contacts" command in QuickBooks Online. The numbers match the steps in this activity.

3. In the window that then opens, the selected contact should appear in the "Merge transactions from" drop-down.
4. Choose the contact with whom to merge from the "Into" drop-down.
5. Click "Merge contacts" to finish.

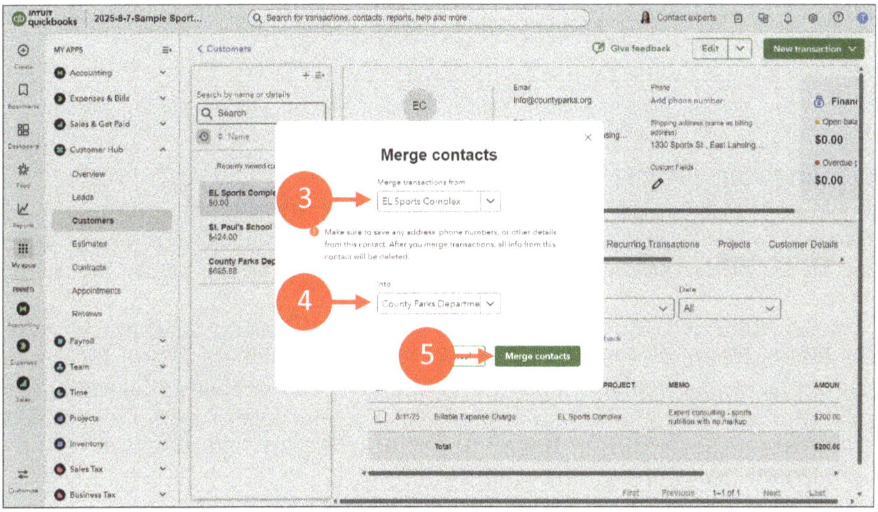

Figure 44: A picture showing how to merge contacts in QuickBooks Online. The numbers match the steps in the preceding activity.

CHAPTER 5- SALES TAX

5.1- Enabling Sales Tax in QuickBooks Online

Collecting and paying sales tax can be tricky. Some companies have to handle multiple sales taxes, and they may sell both taxable and non-taxable items. QuickBooks Online uses an automated sales tax process to make this easier.

In QuickBooks Online Plus, you can apply sales tax to taxable items for taxable customers. It tracks how much sales tax is collected and for which tax agencies. It calculates sales tax based on your company's location, the customer's status and location, or a custom rate you choose. QuickBooks can then create checks for the tax agencies when the taxes are due.

To enable sales tax:

1. Select the "Sales Tax" app in the "All apps" bar.
2. Click the "Overview" link.
3. Click the "Get started" button to open a window where you answer questions and click "Next" to set up sales tax.
4. Enter or confirm your company's address and click "Next."
5. Select the filing frequency for each tax agency and click "Next."
6. Add any other tax agencies if needed and click "Next."
7. When finished, click "Finish and turn on sales tax," then "Done."

After setup, QuickBooks shows your sales tax return information in the "Sales tax returns" page.

In the "Sales tax returns" page:

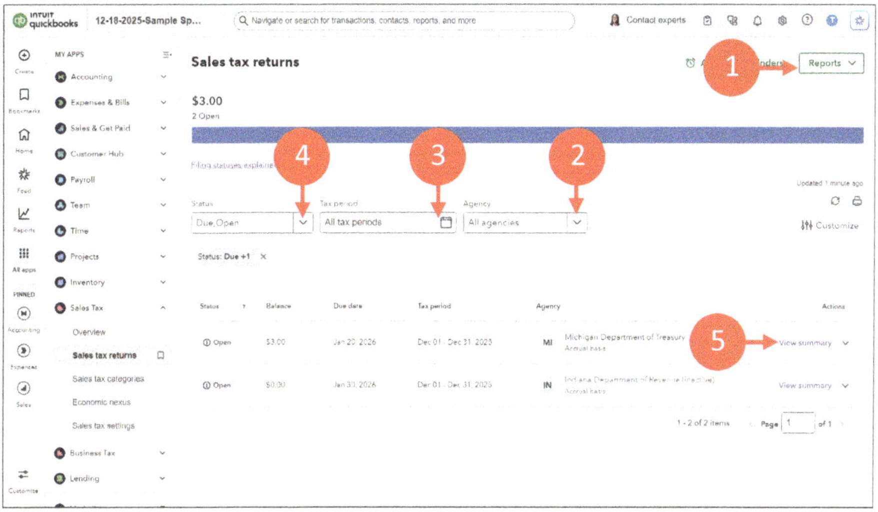

Figure 45: A picture of the Sales tax returns page in QuickBooks Online. The numbers match the steps in this activity.

1. To run sales tax reports, use the "Reports" drop-down.
2. To show tax returns by tax agency, select one from the "Agency" drop-down.
3. To select a sales tax date range to show for the agency, use the "Tax period" drop-down.
4. To filter returns by status, use the "Status" drop-down.
5. To see instructions for completing and recording an agency's sales tax return, click its "View summary" link.

5.2- Changing Sales Tax Agencies in QuickBooks Online

Sales tax agencies in QuickBooks Online are the entities for whom you collect sales tax. There are many possible scenarios in which you need to add, edit, or inactivate your sales tax agencies. You need to add a new sales tax agency if you start collecting sales tax for a new location. You need to edit an existing agency if your sales tax filing frequency changes. If you no longer collect sales tax for an existing sales tax agency, you can inactivate it.

To manage sales tax agencies in QuickBooks Online, select the "Sales Tax" app in the "All apps" bar and then click its "Sales tax settings" link to open the "Sales tax settings" page. You can then perform the following activities on the sales tax agencies in the "Sales tax settings" page.

To add a new sales tax agency:

1. Click the "Add agency" button in the upper-right corner of the "Sales tax settings" page.

2. Select the agency name, filing frequency, start date, and reporting method.
3. Click "Save."

Figure 46: A picture showing how to add an agency in QuickBooks Online. The numbers match the steps in the preceding activity.

To edit an existing tax agency:

1. Click "Edit" in the desired sales tax agency's "Action" column.

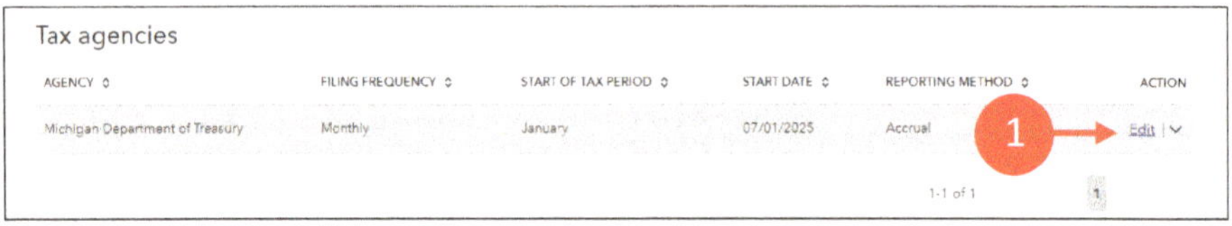

Figure 47: A picture showing how to edit a sales tax agency in QuickBooks Online. The number matches the step in this activity.

2. Change the filing frequency, start date, or reporting method.
3. Click "Save."

To make an agency inactive:

1. Select the "Make inactive" choice from the "Action" column's drop-down for the desired agency.

2. Confirm the action.

To reactivate an inactive agency:

1. Click the "Make active" link in its "Action" column.

5.3- Changing Sales Tax Rates in QuickBooks Online

The "Custom rates" section of the "Sales tax settings" page in QuickBooks Online lets you create and manage custom sales tax rates, if needed. You can create, edit, or inactivate these custom sales tax rates. To open the "Sales tax settings" page, select the "Sales Tax" app in the "All apps" bar and then click its "Sales tax settings" link. Then:

To add a custom sales tax rate:

1. Click drop-down arrow on the "Add agency" button in the upper-right corner of the page and select "Add custom rate."
2. Choose a "Single" or "Combined" rate.
3. Enter the name, agency, and rate, as needed.
4. Click "Save."

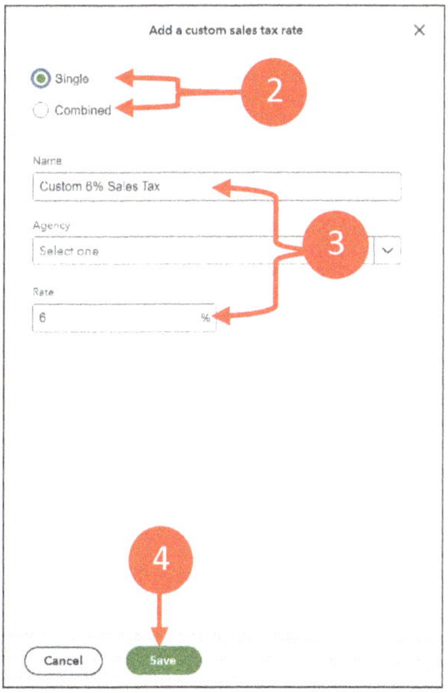

Figure 48: A picture showing how to add a "Single" custom sales tax rate in QuickBooks Online. The numbers match the steps in the preceding activity.

To edit a custom sales tax rate:

1. Click "Edit" in the "Action" column.
2. Make changes and click "Continue."

3. Click "Edit" to finish.

Figure 49: A picture showing how to edit a custom sales tax rate in QuickBooks Online. The number matches the step in this activity.

To make a custom tax rate inactive:

1. Click the drop-down in its "Action" column.
2. Select "Make inactive."

5.4- How to Mark Customers and Items as Taxable or Not Taxable in QuickBooks Online

To use QuickBooks Online for automated sales tax, you must first set up your sales tax agencies and, if needed, any custom sales tax rates. You then enter customer addresses and mark if they are non-taxable. You must then mark your products and services as taxable or non-taxable. QuickBooks Online then automatically calculates and tracks sales tax when you use this information in your sales forms.

To enter customer sales tax location info or mark a customer as non-taxable:

1. Click the "Customers" link in the "Customer Hub" app in the "All apps" bar.
2. Click the name of the customer to edit in the Customers list.
3. Click the "Edit" button in the upper-right corner of the customer details page and enter their billing and shipping addresses in the "Addresses" section of the "Customer" pane.

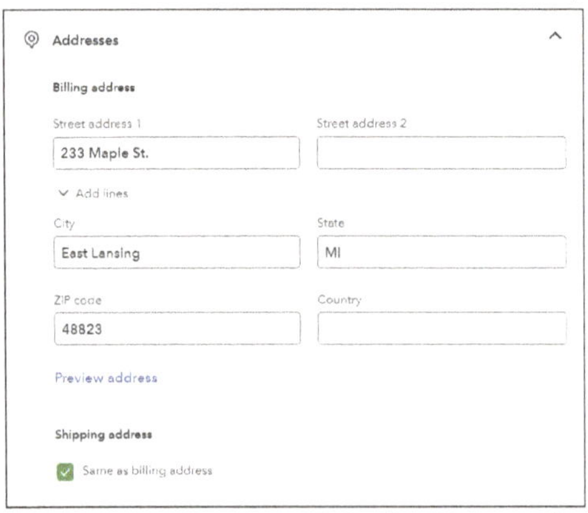

Figure 50: A picture of the "Addresses" section in the "Customers" pane in QuickBooks Online.

4. If needed, to mark them as tax exempt, check the “This customer is tax exempt” checkbox in the "Additional info" section, select a reason for the exemption, and, optionally, enter any exemption details.

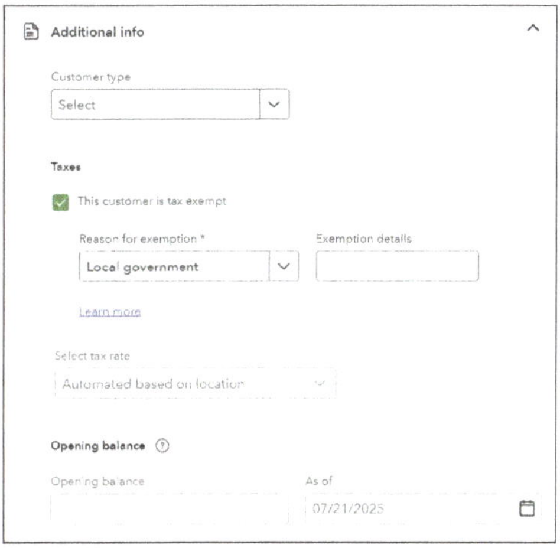

Figure 51: A picture of the "Additional info" section in the "Customer" pane in QuickBooks Online.

5. If needed, to select a custom tax rate, choose it from the "Select tax rate" drop-down in the "Additional info" section.
6. Click “Save” at the bottom of the "Customer" pane.

To mark a product or service as taxable or non-taxable:

1. Click the "Settings" button in the QuickBooks Online toolbar.
2. Click "Products and services" in the menu.
3. Find the product to mark and click "Edit" in its "Action" column.
4. In the pane that opens, select the sales tax category from the "Sales tax category" drop-down in the "Sales" section.

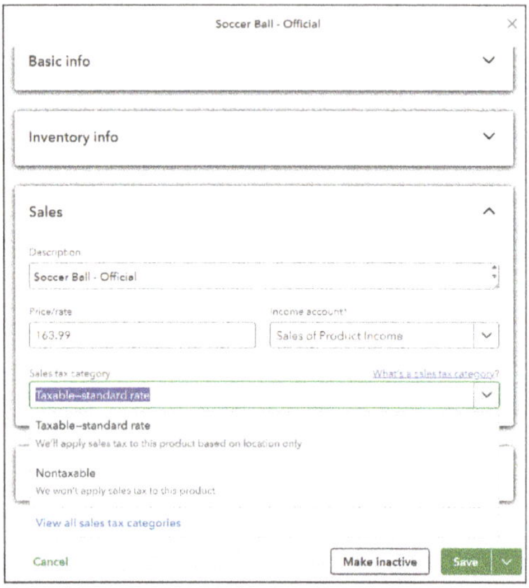

Figure 52: A picture of a user selecting a choice from the "Sales tax category" drop-down in the "Sales" section of a product pane in QuickBooks Online.

5. Click "Save" at the bottom of the pane.

5.5- Creating Sales Tax Reports in QuickBooks Online

The "Sales tax returns" page in QuickBooks Online Plus lets you run sales tax reports and view sales tax return info. To open the "Sales tax returns" page in QuickBooks Online, click the "Sales tax returns" link under the "Sales Tax" app in the "All apps" bar. If using the automatic sales tax feature, you can see the current sales tax due. Select the sales tax agency, tax period, and return status from the drop-down menus.

At the bottom, you'll see sales tax returns by period with statuses like "Paid," "Open," "Due," and "Overdue." Click "View summary" for instructions on recording returns.

To view sales tax reports:

1. Click the "Reports" drop-down in the "Sales tax overview" page.

2. Select the report to run: “Sales tax liability report,” “Taxable customer report,” or “Nontaxable transaction review.”

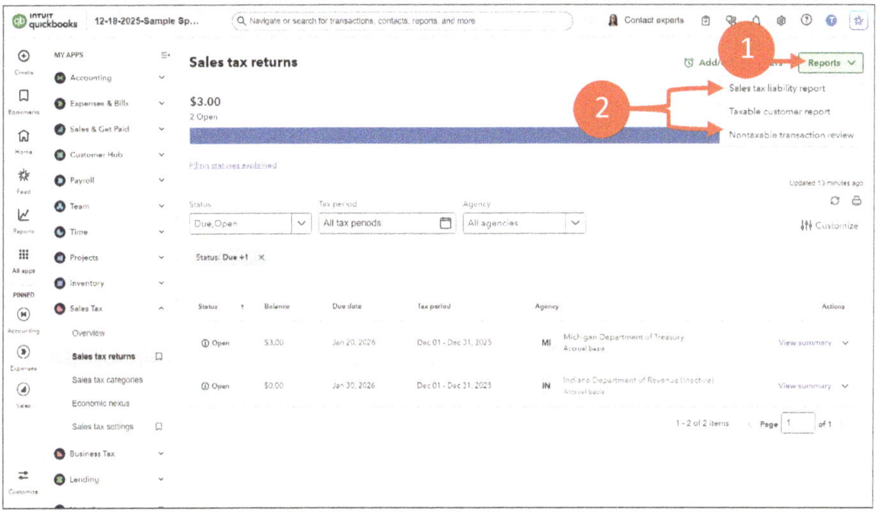

Figure 53: A picture showing how to run the sales tax reports in the "Sales tax overview" page in QuickBooks Online. The numbers match the steps in the preceding activity.

To change the date range in a sales tax report, use the “Report period” drop-down or the date calendar fields.

QuickBooks also provides “Taxable Sales Detail” and “Taxable Sales Summary” reports. To run these:

1. Click “Reports” in the Navigation Bar.
2. Click “Standard reports” in the "Reports & Analytics" bar.
3. Find the “Sales tax” report category in the list of reports.
4. Click either report name in the "Sales tax" category to open it.

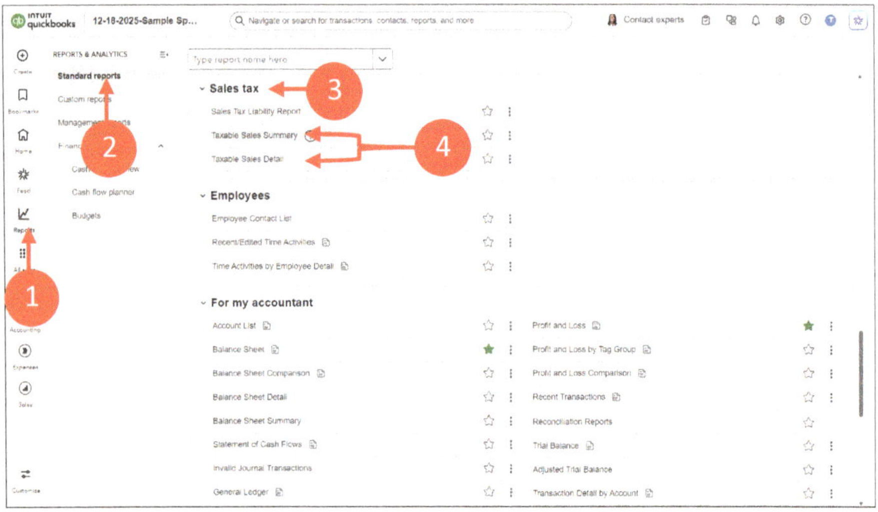

Figure 54: A picture showing how to run the additional sales tax reports within the "Sales tax" reports category in QuickBooks Online. The numbers match the steps in this activity.

5. If needed, change its report settings.
6. Click “Back to standard reports” to return to the report list.

5.6- Paying Sales Tax in QuickBooks Online

You must file a sales tax return and pay the sales tax you collect for each sales tax agency using the filing frequency required for the sales tax. Make sure to follow the instructions for each sales tax to pay the sales tax in real life and record it in QuickBooks, too.

To pay sales tax in QuickBooks Online:

1. Select the “Sales Tax” app in the "All apps" bar and then click its “Sales tax returns” link to open the "Sales tax returns" page.
2. To filter the sales tax returns, use the "Status," "Tax period," and/or “Agency” drop-downs.
3. To pay sales tax for a period, click the “View summary” link for the period and follow the instructions to pay the tax.

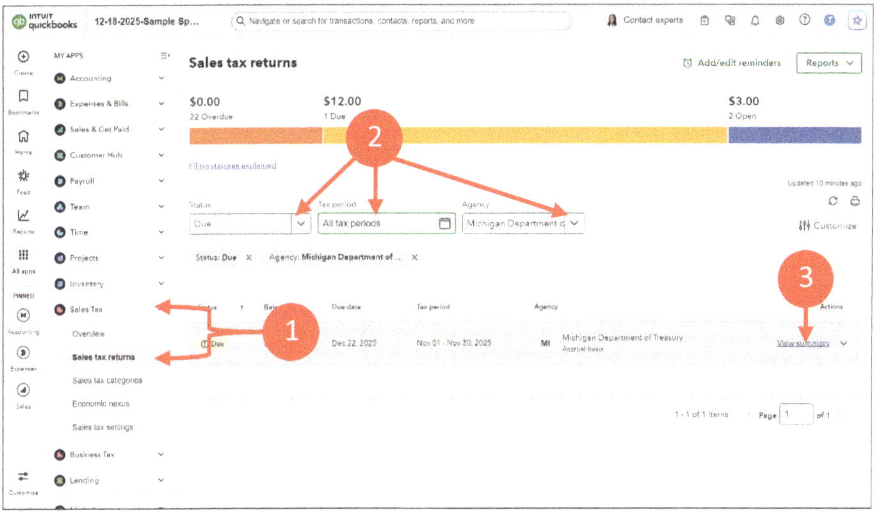

Figure 55: A picture showing how to start to make a sales tax payment in QuickBooks Online from the "Sales Tax overview" page. The numbers match the steps in this activity.

4. If needed, to add a sales tax adjustment, click the “+ Add an adjustment and/or prepayment" link, select the reason, date, account, and amount, and click “Add” to add it.

5. Click the “Record payment” button to continue.

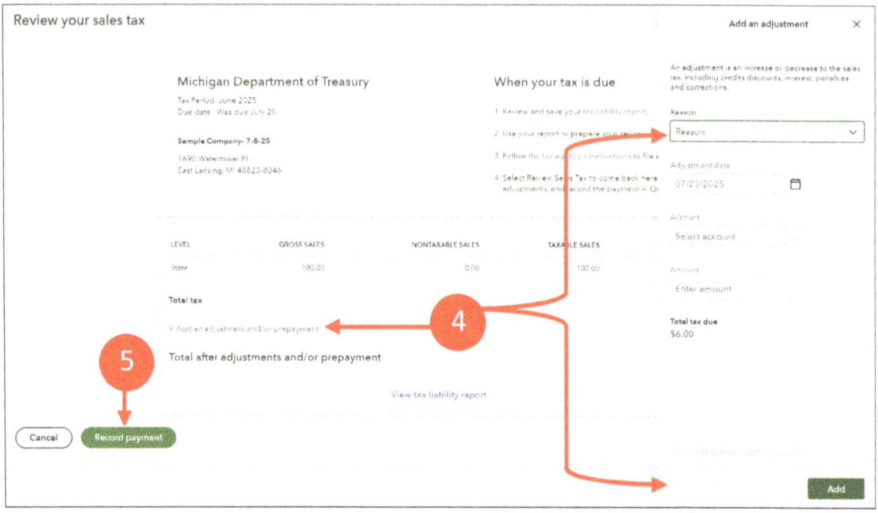

Figure 56: A picture showing how to add an adjustment and/or prepayment to a sales tax payment in QuickBooks Online, if needed. The numbers match the steps in this activity.

6. In the "Record payment" screen, ensure the amount is correct.
7. Select the payment date and bank account.
8. Add a memo, if needed.
9. Check the “Print check” checkbox if you want to print a check.
10. Click the “Record payment” button to finish.

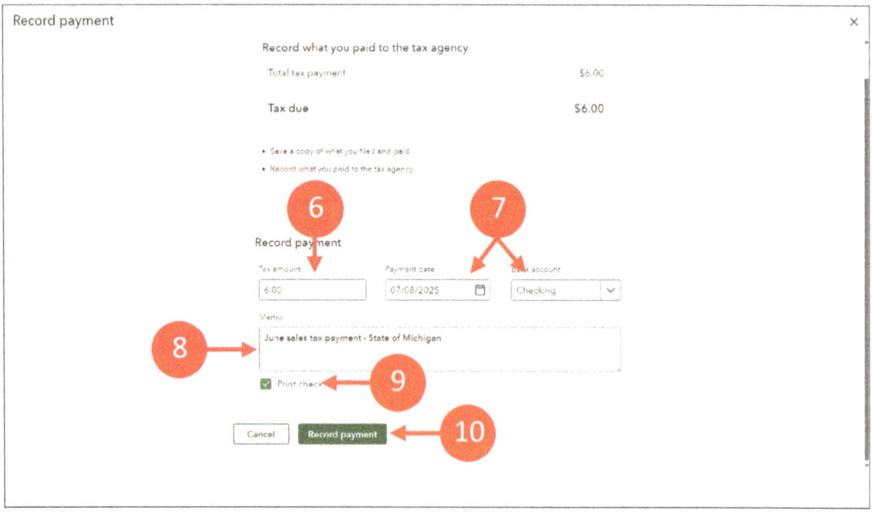

Figure 57: A picture showing how to finish recording a sales tax payment in QuickBooks Online. The numbers match the steps in this activity.

To view the sales tax return later, click the “Review sales tax” link for the sales tax period in the "Sales Tax overview" page.

CHAPTER 6- PRODUCTS AND SERVICES

6.1- Enabling Inventory in QuickBooks Online

In QuickBooks Online, the Products and Services list shows everything you buy or sell. If you have a QuickBooks Plus or Advanced subscription, you can make special products called Inventory items. But first, you need to turn on inventory tracking. This helps you see how much you have and when to order more.

To track inventory in QuickBooks Online:

1. Click the "Settings" button in the QuickBooks Online toolbar.
2. Click "Account and settings" under "Your Company."
3. Click "Sales" to the left, then "Products and services" to the right.
4. Turn on "Track quantity and price/rate" and "Track inventory quantity on hand" and select an "Inventory valuation method," if needed, but note you cannot change this selection later.
5. Click "Save" and then "Done."

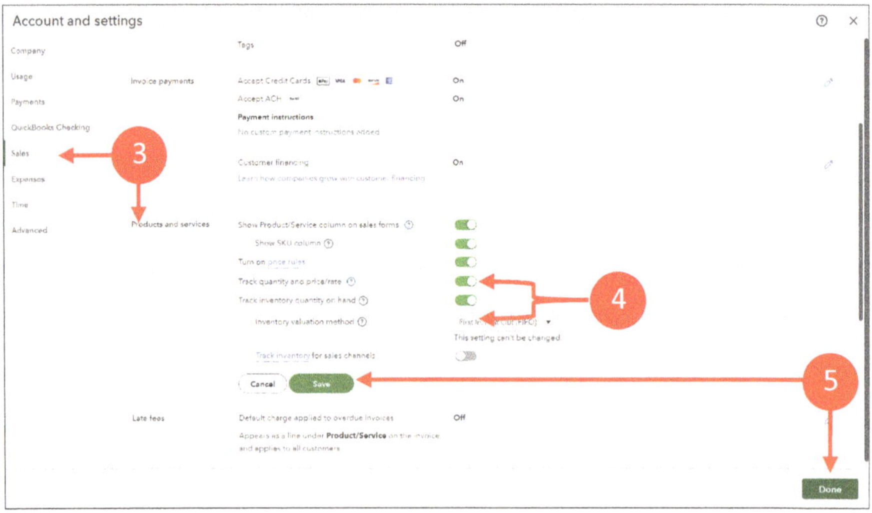

Figure 58: A picture showing how to enable inventory in QuickBooks Online. The numbers match the steps in the preceding activity.

This adds "Quantity" and "Rate" fields to sales forms and tracks stock levels and costs. QuickBooks will update inventory when you buy or sell items.

6.2- Creating a New Inventory Item in QuickBooks Online

QuickBooks Online keeps track of the products and services you sell in its Products and services list. When you create a new product or service, you must choose an "item type." The options are:

- **Inventory item**: Products you buy or sell and for which you track quantities.
- **Non-inventory item**: Products you buy or sell but for which you don't track quantities.
- **Service**: Services your company provides.
- **Bundle**: Items you sell together as a set.

To create Inventory items in QuickBooks Online Plus:

1. Click the "Settings" button in the QuickBooks Online toolbar.
2. Click "Products and services" under "Lists."
3. To add your first item, click the "Add an item" button in the page to open a product/service pane.
4. To add all future items, click "New" in this page and select "Inventory item" to open a product/service pane.
5. In the "Basic info" section at the top of this pane:
    a. Enter the item name.
    b. If needed, select "Inventory item" from the "Item type" drop-down.
    c. Optionally, enter the SKU and add an image.
    d. Optionally, select a category or create a new one.

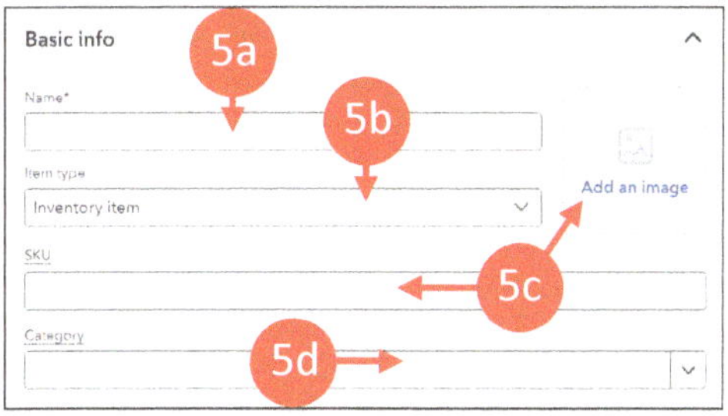

Figure 59: A picture of the fields in the "Basic info" section of the pane. The numbers and letters match the steps in this activity.

6. In the "Inventory info" section:

a. Enter the initial quantity on hand and the date.
b. If desired, enter the reorder point.
c. Select the inventory asset account.

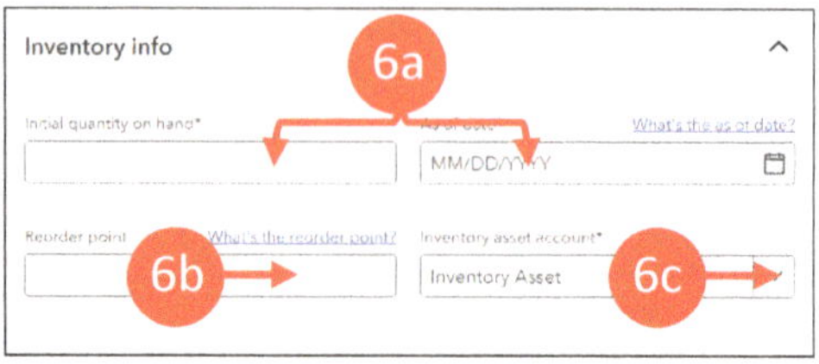

Figure 60: A picture of the "Inventory info" section in the pane. The numbers and letters match the steps in this activity.

7. In the “Sales” section:
    a. Enter a description for sales forms.
    b. Enter the default sales price.
    c. Select the income account.
    d. Select the sales tax category if needed.

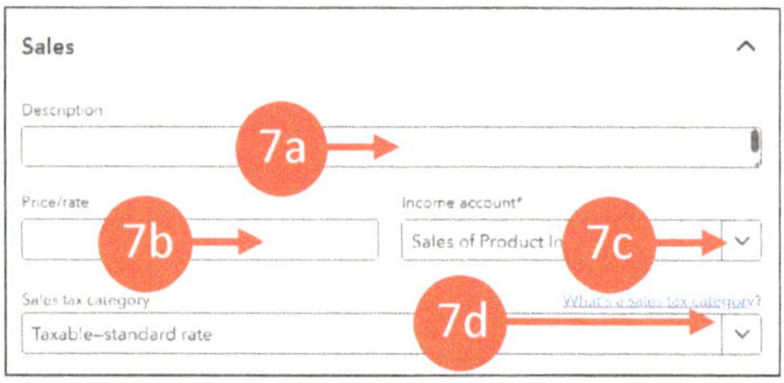

Figure 61: A picture of the "Sales" section in the pane. The numbers and letters match the steps in this activity.

8. In the “Purchasing” section:
    a. Enter a description for purchase forms.
    b. Enter the default purchase price.
    c. Select the expense account.

d. Select a preferred vendor if needed.

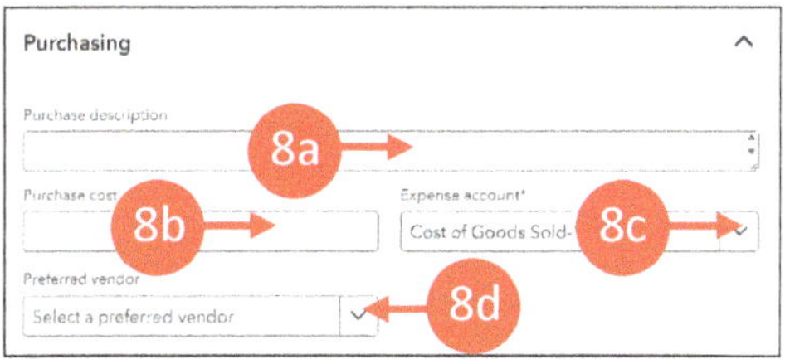

Figure 62: A picture of the "Purchasing" section in the pane. The numbers and letters match the steps in this activity.

9. To finish, click one of the buttons at the bottom of the pane:
    a. Click "Save and close" to save and then close the pane.
    b. Click "Save and new" to save and then add another item.
    c. Click "Cancel" to discard the item.

Once inventory tracking is enabled for an item, it cannot be turned off. To disable tracking, inactivate the item and create a new one.

6.3- Creating a New Non-inventory Item or Service in QuickBooks Online

You create non-inventory items in the Products and services list in QuickBooks Online for products you buy and/or sell, but for which you don't need to track inventory. Similarly, you create Service items in the same list for services your company provides.

To create a Non-inventory or Service item in QuickBooks Online:

1. Click the "Settings" button in the QuickBooks Online toolbar.
2. Click "Products and services" under "Lists."
3. To add your first item, click the "Add an item" button in the page to open a product/service pane.
4. To add all future items, click "New" in this page and select either "Non-inventory item" or "Service" to open a product/service pane.
5. In the "Basic info" section at the top of this pane:
    a. Enter the item name.
    d. If needed, select "Non-inventory item" or "Service" from the "Item type" drop-down.
    e. Optionally, enter the SKU and add an image.

b. Optionally, select a category or create a new one.

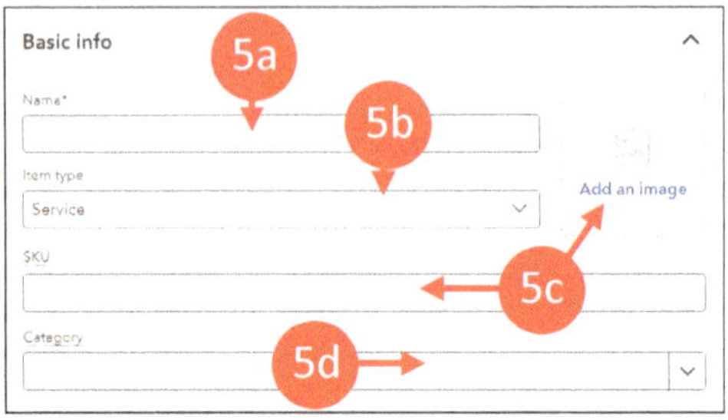

Figure 63: A picture of the fields in the "Basic info" section of the pane. The numbers and letters match the steps in this activity.

6. In the "Sales" section:
    a. To sell the item, check "I sell this product/service to my customers."
    b. Enter a description for sales forms.
    c. Enter the default sales price.
    d. Select the income account.
    e. Select the sales tax category if needed.

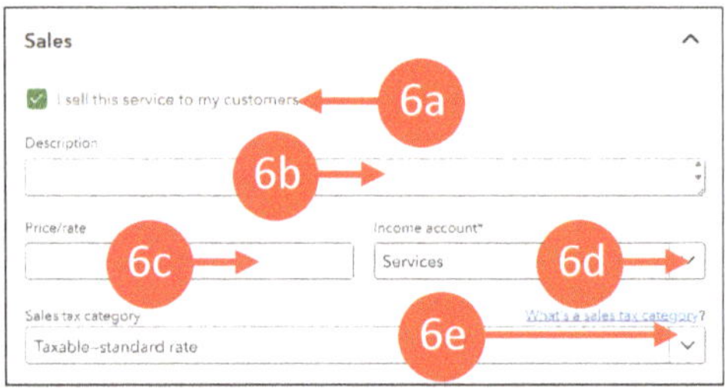

Figure 64: A picture of the "Sales" section in the pane. The numbers and letters match the steps in this activity.

7. In the "Purchasing" section:
    a. To buy the item, check "I purchase this from a vendor."
    b. Enter a description for purchase forms.
    c. Enter the default purchase price.
    d. Select the expense account.

e. Select a preferred vendor if needed.

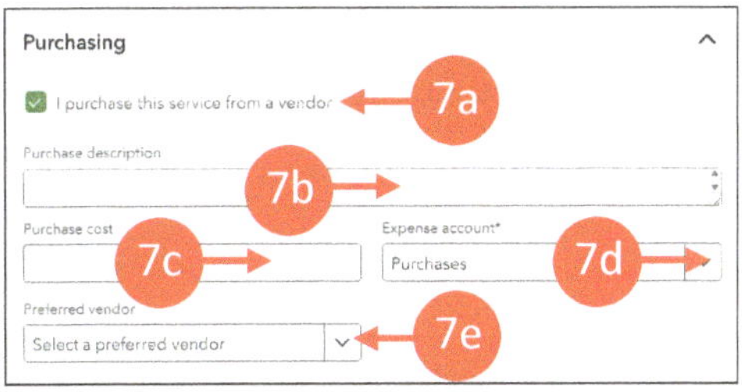

Figure 65: A picture of the "Purchasing" section in the pane. The numbers and letters match the steps in this activity.

8. To finish, click one of the buttons at the bottom of the pane:
    a. Click "Save and close" to save and then close the pane.
    b. Click "Save and new" to save and then add another item.
    c. Click "Cancel" to discard item.

6.4- Creating a New Bundle Item in QuickBooks Online

A bundle item in QuickBooks Online contains other, existing product and service items you sell together as a set. So, before you create the bundle item, you must first create its component items in the Products and services list. After you do that, you can then create the bundle item.

To create a Bundle item in QuickBooks Online:

1. Create the items to include in the bundle within the Products and services list, first.
2. Click the "Settings" button in the QuickBooks Online toolbar.
3. Click "Products and services" under "Lists."
4. To add your first item, click the "Add an item" button in the page to open a product/service pane.
5. To add all future items, click "New" in this page and select "Bundle" to open a product/service pane.
6. In the "Basic info" section at the top of this pane:
    a. Enter the item name.
    b. If needed, select "Bundle" from the "Item type" drop-down.
    c. Optionally, enter the SKU and add an image.
7. In the "Sales" section:
    a. Enter a description for sales forms.
8. In the "Items included in the bundle" section:

a. Optionally, to show individual items in the bundle, check "Display bundle items when printing or sending transactions."

b. To add items to the bundle:

    i. Click a row and then select an item from the drop-down.

    ii. Enter the quantity for the item.

    iii. Repeat the two previous steps to add all the items to the bundle.

c. To manage the bundle's items:

    i. Click the trash can icon to remove items.

    ii. Click "Add lines" to add lines for more items.

    iii. Drag an item up or down by the 6-dot handle to its left to change its order in the list.

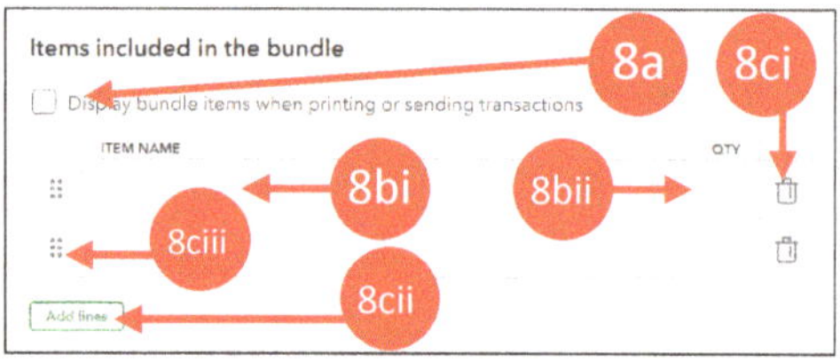

Figure 66: A picture of the "Items included in the bundle" section of the pane. The numbers and letters match the steps in this activity.

9. To finish, do one of the following:
    a. Click "Save and close" to save and then close the pane.
    b. Click "Save and new" to save and then add another item.
    c. Click "Cancel" to discard changes.

6.5- Entering a Purchase Order in QuickBooks Online

Purchase orders in QuickBooks Online let you order products from vendors. When the items arrive, you can then enter a bill for the received items.

How to create a purchase order in QuickBooks Online:

1. Hover over the "+ Create" button.
2. Select "Purchase order" under "Vendors."
3. Select a vendor from the "Vendor" drop-down.
    a. To add a new vendor, select "Add new," enter their details, and save it.

4. The selected vendor's information then fills in the vendor fields at the top of the purchase order form, but you can change these values, if needed.
    a. If needed, enter the vendor's "Email."
    b. Optionally, to add Cc or Bcc email addresses, click the "Cc/Bcc" link, enter email addresses, and click "Done."
    c. Enter the vendor's "Mailing address."
    d. Optionally, to drop ship to a customer, select the customer from the "Ship to" drop-down.
    e. Your address or the customer's address (for drop shipments) should appear in the "Shipping address" field.
    f. If needed, select the correct "Purchase Order date."
    g. Optionally, to set a shipping preference, select it from the "Ship Via" field.
    h. Optionally, enter any custom fields, location, or permit number fields.

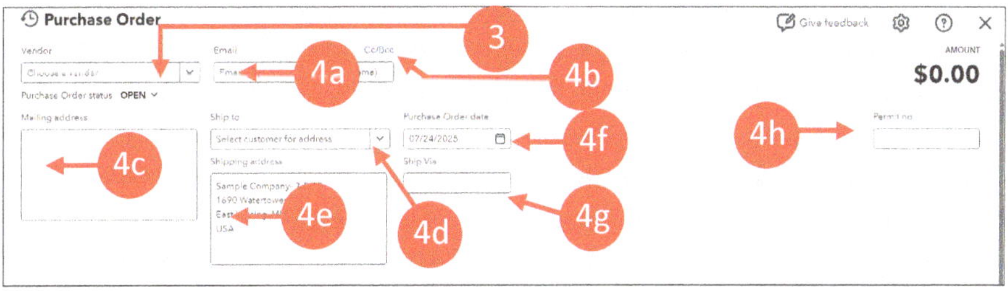

Figure 67: A picture of the upper part of the "Purchase Order" form in QuickBooks Online. The numbers and letters match the steps in this activity.

5. Enter the purchase order's line items in the Category details and/or Item details sections:
    a. If needed, to manually enter purchases, use the line items in the "Category details" section.
        i. For each line, choose the account and enter the purchase description and amount.
        ii. This is the default section if you do not enable showing items in purchase and expense forms.
        iii. This section is rarely used in purchase orders, as it defeats the purpose of receiving inventory items using a purchase order.

b. Alternatively, to select items from your products and services list, use the line items in the "Item details" section.
   i. Select a line item from the "Product/Service" drop-down.
   ii. Optionally, if SKUs are enabled, check the "SKU" field's value.
   iii. Ensure the value in the "Description" field is accurate.
   iv. Enter the quantity and rate into the "Quantity" and "Rate" fields to calculate the amount, shown in the "Amount" field.
   v. Optionally, to assign each item to a customer/project or class, if enabled, use the "Customer/Project" and "Class" drop-down fields.

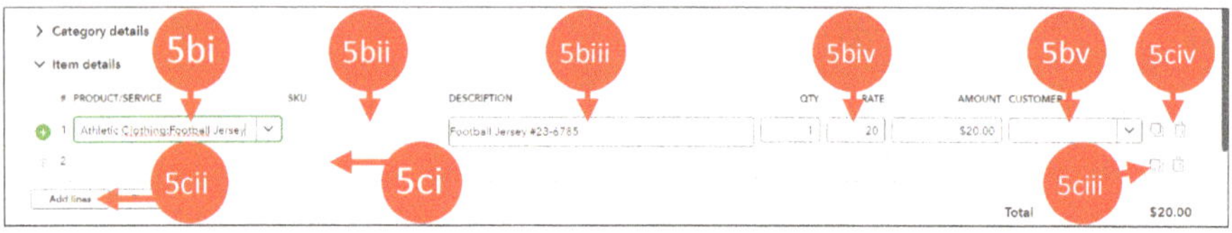

Figure 68: picture of the "Item details" section in the "Purchase Order" window in QuickBooks Online. The numbers and letters match the steps in this activity.

c. To add or delete lines in the Category details and Item details sections:
   i. Click into the last line to add a new line.
   ii. Click "Add lines" to add multiple lines.
   iii. To copy a line, click the copy icon at its right end.
   iv. Click the trash can icon to delete a line.

6. Optionally, to add messages and attachments to the purchase order:
   a. Type a message to the vendor in "Your message to vendor" field.
   b. Add a memo for yourself in the "Memo" field.

c. Attach files up to 20MB using the "Attachments" field.

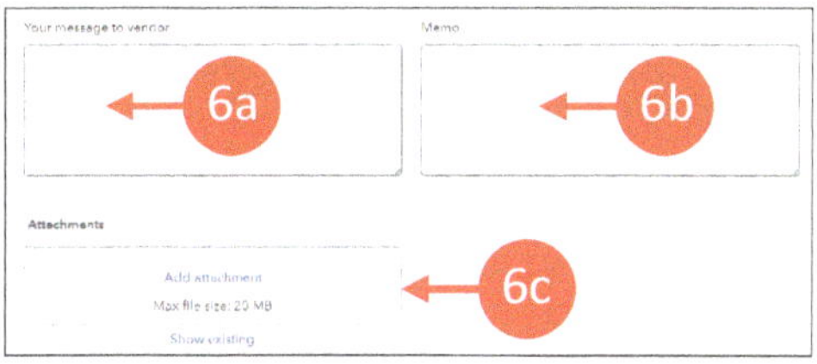

Figure 69: A picture of the message and attachments fields in the "Purchase Order" form in QuickBooks Online. The numbers and letters match the steps in this activity.

7. To finish, select a choice from the toolbar at the bottom of the purchase order:
    a. To cancel the purchase order, click the "Cancel" button.
    b. To clear all data from the current purchase order, click the "Clear" button.
    c. To save and print the purchase order, click the "Print" button.
    d. To save the purchase order, click the "Save" button.
    e. To save the purchase order and then send it, close the window, or create a new purchase order, click the corresponding choice from the "Save and Send" drop-down button.

Figure 70: A picture of the toolbar at the bottom of the "Purchase Order" window in QuickBooks Online. The numbers and letters match the steps in the preceding activity.

6.6- Adding Custom Fields to Sales and Purchasing Forms in QuickBooks Online

You can create custom fields in QuickBooks Online for customers and/or transactions. This helps you tag customers and/or transactions with custom information you need for your company. Depending on the custom field's category, you enter custom field data either once per customer or once per transaction, not per line item in a transaction.

To create custom fields in QuickBooks Online:

1. Click the “Settings” button in the QuickBooks Online toolbar and select “Custom fields” under “Lists.”
2. To add a new field, click “Add custom field” or “Add field” in the page that opens.
3. In the "Add custom field" pane that opens:
    a. Type a name for the custom field.
    b. Select the type of data it contains from the "Data type" drop-down.
        i. If you select "Dropdown list," then select a color (for "Customer" category fields only), enter the drop-down values into the "Dropdown list item" column, and ensure the "Active" checkbox for each is checked to have it appear in the drop-down.
    c. To choose the custom field category, select either "Customer," "Transaction," or, if available, "Time." Customer custom fields appear in customer records and, if desired, within customer forms. Transaction custom fields appear within the selected transaction forms. Time fields appear in timesheet in QuickBooks Time.
    d. To add the custom field to transaction forms, check the checkbox for the desired forms under the "Select forms" column.

e. To also print the custom field on a transaction form, if available, click its "Print on form" toggle switch.

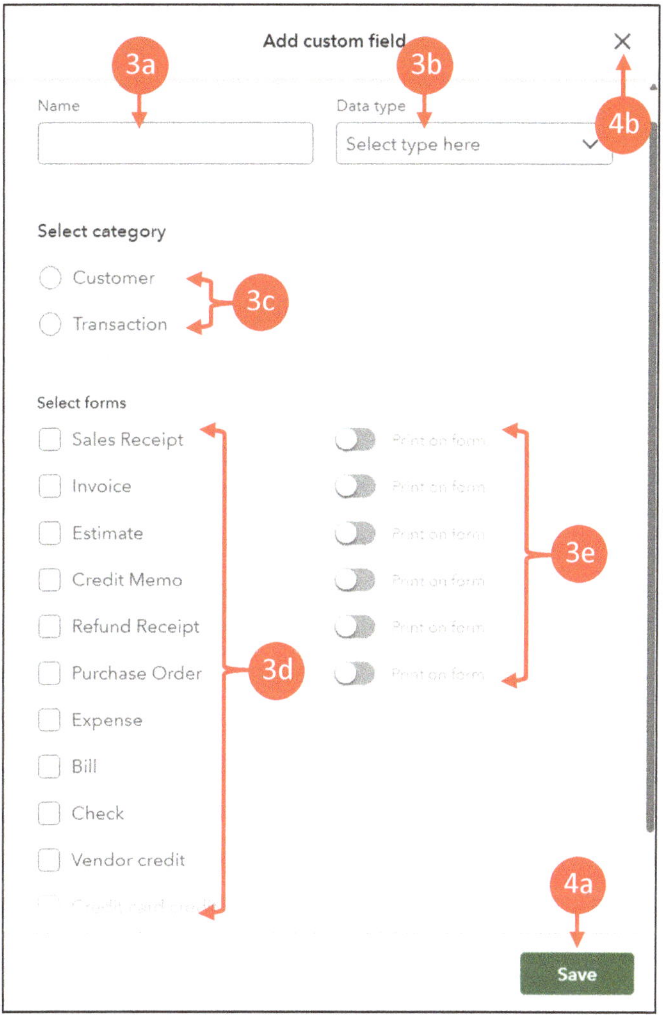

Figure 71: A picture of the "Add custom field" pane in QuickBooks Online. The numbers and letters match the steps in the activity.

4. To finish:
    a. Click "Save" to save the custom field.
    b. Click "X" to cancel it.

6.7- Adjusting Inventory in QuickBooks Online

While QuickBooks Online tracks inventory through its sales, purchase, and expense forms, sometimes external events happen that change inventory quantities. You can enter an inventory adjustment in QuickBooks Online to account for loss or spoilage of inventory. If needed, you can also adjust the starting values for inventory items when creating a new company file to correct data entry errors made when creating these items and entering the initial inventory on hand.

How to adjust inventory in QuickBooks Online:

1. Click the "Settings" button in the QuickBooks Online toolbar.
2. Select "Products and services" under "Lists" to open the Products and services list.
3. Find the inventory item to adjust in this list and click "Edit" in its "Action" column.
4. To adjust its quantity:
    a. In the "Inventory info" section of the pane that opens, click the "Quantity" link.
    b. Enter the adjustment date.
    c. Choose a reason for the adjustment.
    d. If needed, select the correct "Inventory adjustment account" for the adjustment.
    e. Either enter the new quantity or enter the change in quantity (use negative number for loss).
    f. Add a memo if needed.
    g. Click "Save and close."

Figure 72: A picture showing how to enter an inventory quantity adjustment in QuickBooks Online. The numbers and letters match the steps in this activity.

5. Alternatively, to adjust its starting value, if needed:

a. In the "Inventory info" section of the pane that opens, click the "Starting value" link.

b. Enter the correct initial quantity, cost, and date.

c. Select the correct account.

d. Add a memo if needed.

e. Click "Save."

Figure 73: A picture showing how to make an inventory starting value adjustment in QuickBooks Online. The numbers and letters match the steps in this activity.

f. If you're unsure of the accuracy of your "starting value" inventory adjustment, it's best to check it with your accountant.

6.8- Creating a Discount Line Item in QuickBooks Online

QuickBooks Online lets you give discounts to customers in sales forms. You can turn on the "Discount" field in sales forms to add a percentage or amount discount to the **total** in sales forms. Alternatively, to apply a discount to **specific items or subtotaled amounts** in sales forms, you can create and use a discount line item.

To apply a discount to a total if you enable the "Discount" field in sales forms in QuickBooks Online:

1. Fill in the sales form, as usual.
2. Below the line item area, use the "Discount" toggle switch or drop-down to choose a percentage or value.
3. Then enter the discount amount or percentage into the adjacent field.

4. Finish the sales form, as usual.

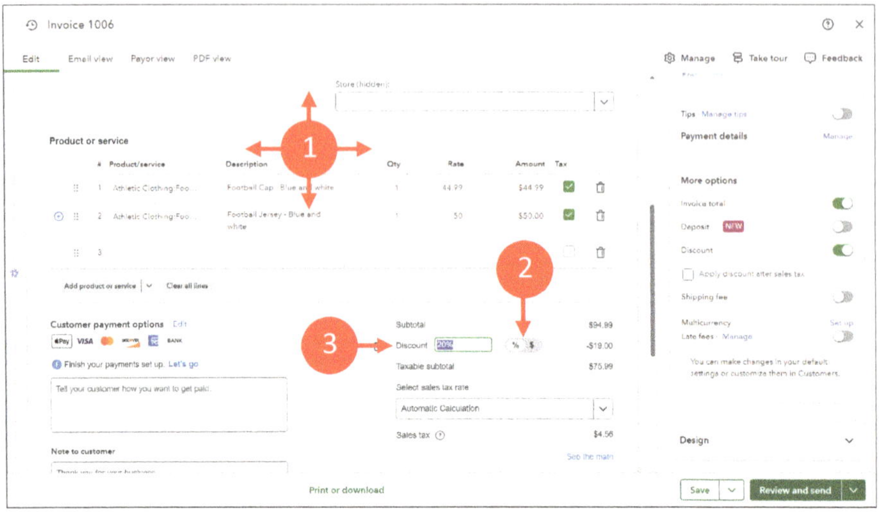

Figure 74: A picture of a user applying a discount to a total within an invoice in QuickBooks Online. The numbers match the steps in the preceding activity.

Alternatively, to create a Discount line item to discount line items or subtotals in sales forms:

1. Click the “Settings” button in the QuickBooks Online toolbar.
2. Select “Products and services” under “Lists.”
3. Click “New” and choose “Non-inventory item.”
4. In the “Basic info” section of the pane, enter the item name (e.g., “Discount-20%”).
5. In the “Sales” section, type the discount's default description to show in sales forms into the "Description" field.
6. Then enter the discount amount as a negative value in the “Price/rate” field.
    a. For a flat discount amount, enter the amount to discount as a negative value.
    b. Alternatively, for a percentage discount, enter the discount percentage as a negative decimal amount. For example, to create a 20% discount, enter “-0.20” as its value.
7. Change the “Income account” to “Discounts given.”
8. Select the correct “Sales tax category.”

9. Click “Save.”

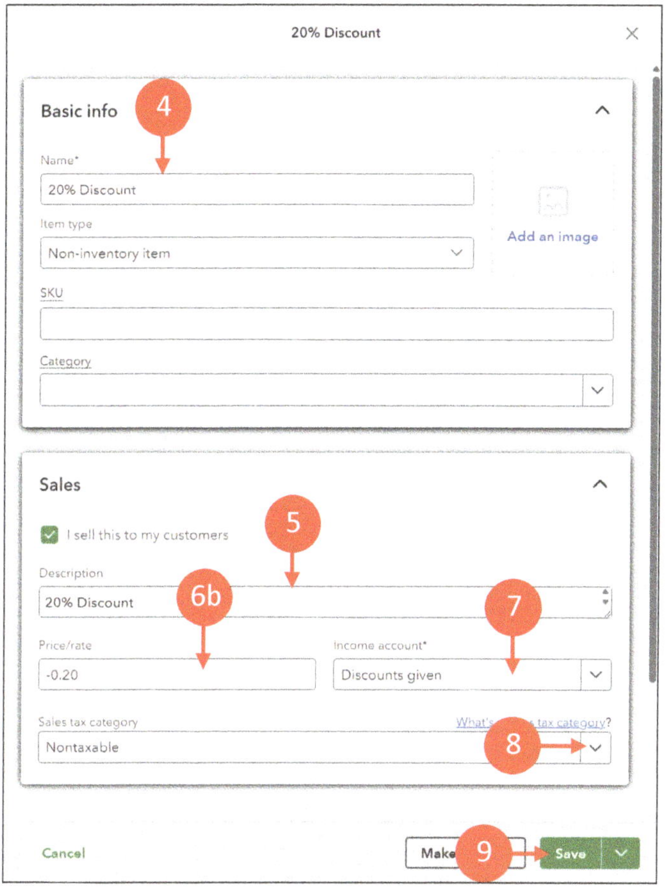

Figure 75: A picture of a user creating a 20% Discount line item to use in sales forms in QuickBooks Online. The numbers and letters match the steps in the preceding activity.

To then use a Discount line item to discount line items or subtotals in sales forms:

1. Hover over the “+ Create” button in the Navigation Bar.
2. Select “Invoice” or “Sales Receipt,” as needed.
3. Choose a customer.
4. **For percentage discounts**, add **only** the line items for the products/services to discount and enter their quantities, rates, and amounts.
    a. Then either add a subtotal line item or note the subtotal amount in the Totals area.

   b. Then add the "Discount" line item and enter the subtotal amount into the "QTY" column for the discount line item.

5. **Alternatively, for flat amount discounts**, add the line items as you wish, enter the "Discount" line item, and enter the discount amount in the "Rate" field as a negative number with a "Qty" of 1 for the discount item.
6. When using a "Discount" line item, it's best to check the sales tax amount to ensure the sales tax calculation is correct.
   a. Adjust the "Tax" checkbox for the discount item if needed.
7. Finally, choose one of the "Save" options to save the transaction.

Figure 76: A picture showing how to apply a percentage-based Discount line item in an invoice in QuickBooks Online. The numbers and letters match the steps in the preceding activity.

6.9- Creating a Payment Line Item in QuickBooks Online

QuickBooks Online doesn't let you record different payment types in one sales receipt. But you can create a payment line item to fix this. For example, if a customer wants to pay by check and cash, you can use a "Payment" item and enter a negative amount in its "Rate" column and then record the remainder of the payment, as usual, to record both payment types in one sales form.

How to create and use a Payment line item in QuickBooks Online:

1. To create the Payment line item:
   a. Click the "Settings" button in the QuickBooks Online toolbar.
   b. Select "Products and services" under "Lists."
   c. Click "New" and choose "Non-inventory item."

d. In the "Basic info" section at the top of this pane, enter the item's name (e.g., "Cash Payment" or "Check Payment").
e. In the "Sales" section, type the same name in the "Description" field.
f. Choose the asset account into which to deposit the funds (e.g., "Cash" or "Payments to deposit") from the "Income account" drop-down.
g. Select "Nontaxable" from the "Sales tax category" drop-down.
h. Click "Save" to save the Payment line item.

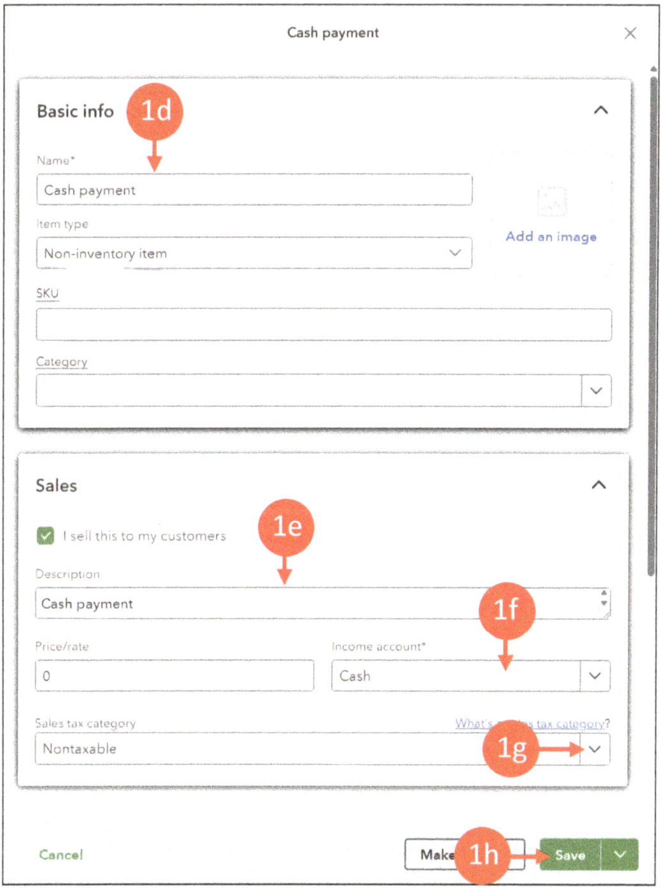

Figure 77: A picture of a user creating a Payment line item in QuickBooks Online. The numbers and letters match the steps in the preceding activity.

2. To use the Payment line item within a sales form:
    a. Fill in the sales form with the customer and line item information, as usual.
    b. Select the Payment line item and enter a quantity of "1" in the "QTY" column.
    c. Then enter a negative amount in the "Rate" column.
    d. Finish and save the sales form, as usual.

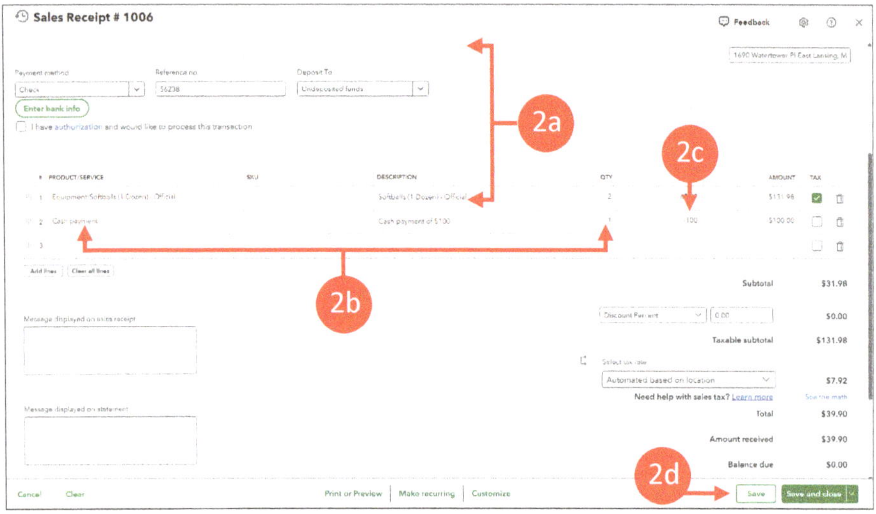

Figure 78: A picture showing how to use a Payment line item in a sales receipt in QuickBooks Online. The numbers and letters match the steps in the preceding activity.

CHAPTER 7- ENTERING SALES

7.1- Entering Invoices in QuickBooks Online

You enter invoices in QuickBooks Online to record customer sales for which you expect payment in the future. The customer's terms set the invoice's payment due date.

How to create an invoice in QuickBooks Online:

1. Hover over the "+ Create" button in the Navigation Bar.
2. Select "Invoice" under "Customers."
3. Select a customer from the "Customer" drop-down or select "Add new" and enter their information and click "Save" in the pane that opens.
4. The customer's information fills in the fields at the top of the form, but you can change these values, if needed.
    a. If needed, enter the "Customer email."
    b. Optionally, to add Cc or Bcc email addresses, click the "Cc/Bcc" link, enter email addresses, and click "Save."
    c. Ensure the "Bill to" shows the customer's billing address and change it if needed.
    d. If you enabled shipping, the invoice shows the "Ship to," "Ship from (hidden)," "Ship via," "Shipping date," and "Tracking no." fields.
        i. Ensure the "Ship to" field shows the customer's default shipping address, which is used for automatic sales tax calculations.
            1. If empty, QuickBooks Online uses the "Ship from (hidden)" field's value or the default company address, instead.
            2. You can change the "Ship from (hidden)" field's address, if needed.
        ii. Check the values for all shipping fields, as needed.

e. The "Invoice no" field shows the next available invoice number, which you can change if you enabled custom transaction numbers in sales forms.

f. The customer's terms appear in the "Terms" field, which you can change.

g. Check and change the "Invoice date," if needed.

h. Check and change the "Due date," if needed.

i. Optionally, enter any custom fields, location, or class per transaction fields if you enabled them.

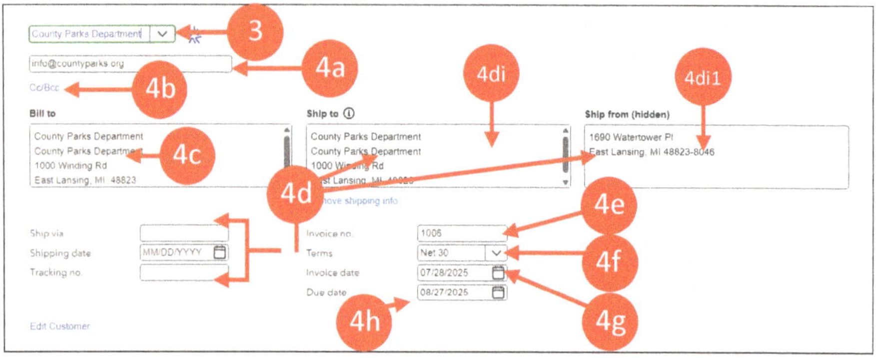

Figure 79: A picture showing some of the fields that may appear at the top of an invoice in QuickBooks Online. The numbers and letters match the steps in this activity.

5. To change common invoice settings, click the "Manage" button in the top toolbar to show a pane at the right side of the invoice.

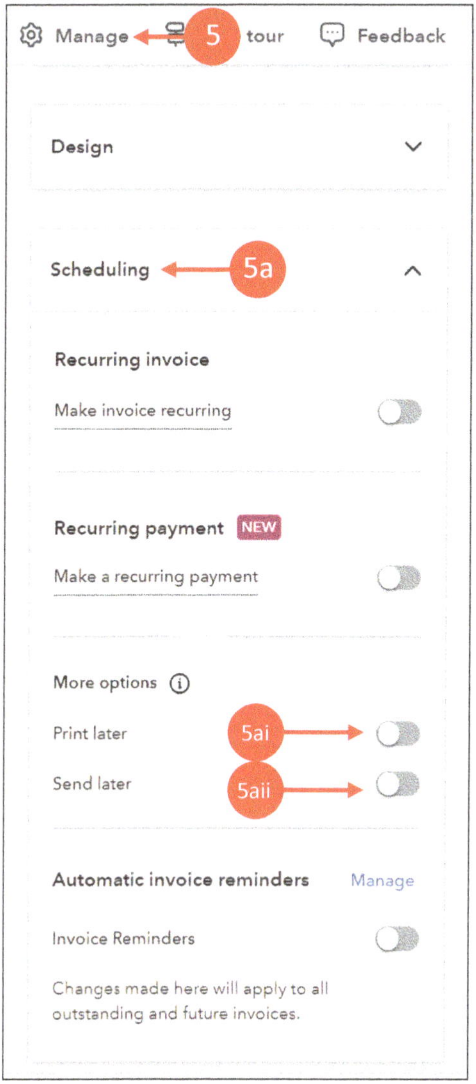

Figure 80: A picture of the "Scheduling" options for an invoice in QuickBooks Online. The numbers and letters match the steps in this activity.

   a. To mark the invoice to print or email later, click the "Scheduling" section to expand it, if needed.
      i. To mark the invoice to print later, click the "Print later" toggle switch to toggle it "On."

ii. To mark the invoice to email later, click the "Send later" toggle switch to toggle it "On."

b. To change payment options, click to expand the "Payment options" section.

i. Click to toggle the payment options on or off for this invoice, as desired.

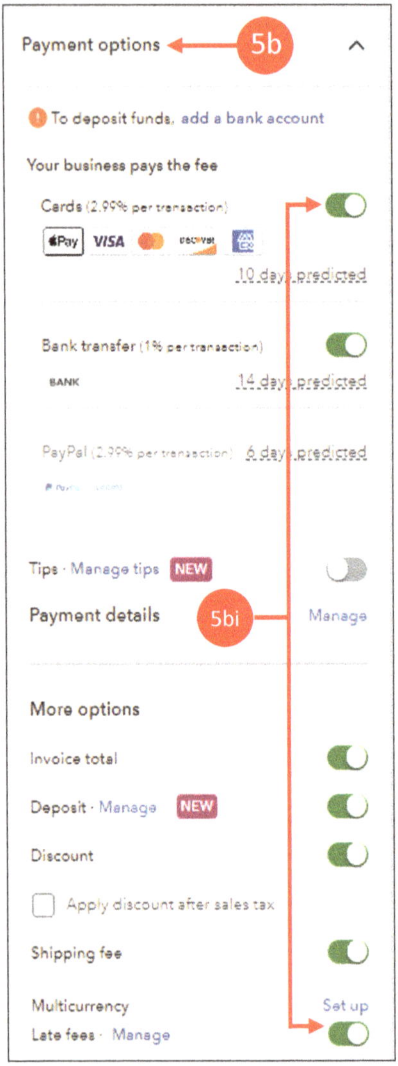

Figure 81: A picture of the "Payment options" for an invoice in QuickBooks Online. The numbers and letters match the steps in this activity.

6. Enter all the line items details for the invoice. Repeat this for each line item row:

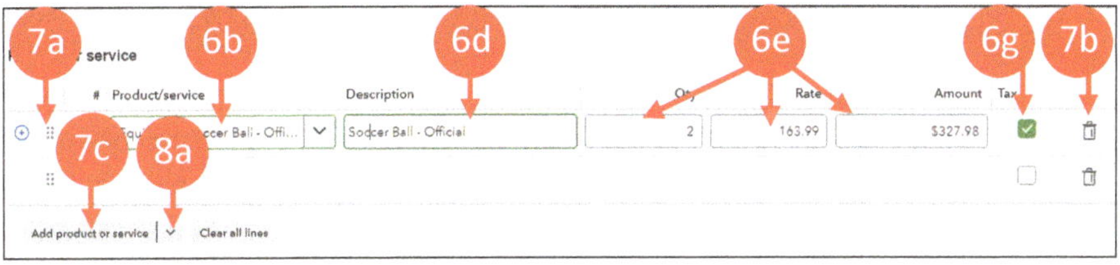

Figure 82: A picture of the line items section in an invoice in QuickBooks Online. The numbers and letters match the steps in this activity.

   a. To select a service date, if enabled, use the "Service Date" field.
   b. To select an item from the Products and services list, use the "Product/Service" drop-down.
   c. Optionally, if SKUs are enabled, check the "SKU" field's value.
   d. Check the value in the "Description" field and change it if needed.
   e. If you enabled quantity and rate fields in sales forms, then enter the quantity and rate into the "Quantity" and "Rate" fields to calculate the amount in the "Amount" field.
      i. Alternatively, if you select a product or service without a rate or quantity or didn't enable them, then enter the total amount into the "Amount" field, if needed.
   f. Optionally, to assign each item a class if you enabled classes per row, use the "Class" drop-down.
   g. If the product or service is taxable, ensure the "Tax" checkbox is checked.
      i. You can check or uncheck this to mark it as taxable or non-taxable.
7. To manage the line items:
   a. To move a line item up or down, click and drag it by the handle at its left end.
   b. To delete a line item, click the "Delete" button at its right end.

   c. To add a new row, either click into the bottom row or click the “Add product or service” button under the rows.

8. Optionally, to add a subtotal, click into the row above the row where you want to insert a subtotal row.
   a. Then click the drop-down on the "Add product or service" button below all the rows and select “Add subtotal.”
9. Optionally, enter any messages or attachments:

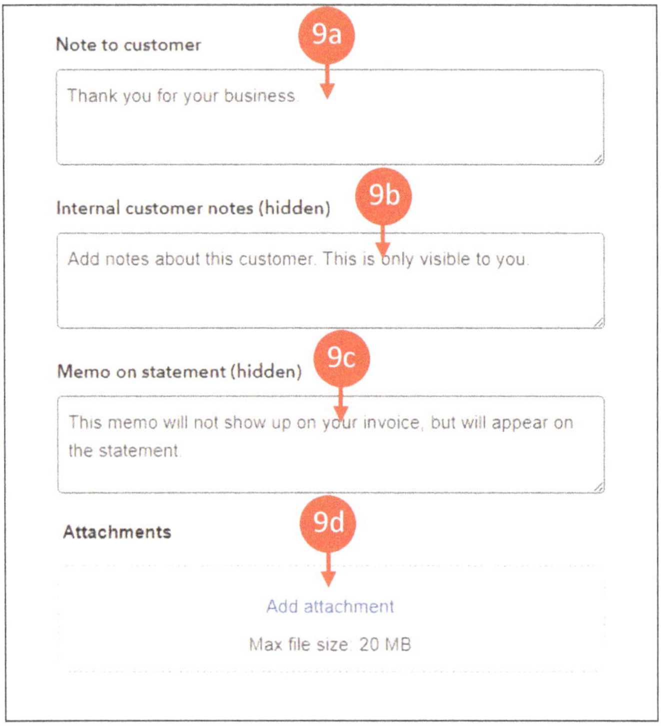

Figure 83: A picture of the messages and attachments area in an invoice in QuickBooks Online. The numbers and letters match the steps in this activity.

   a. To enter a message shown in the form, type it into the “Note to customer” field.
   b. To type hidden internal notes about the customer, type them into the “Internal customer notes (hidden)” field.
   c. To enter a message shown for this invoice in the customer’s statement, type it into the “Memo on statement (hidden)” field.

   d. To attach a file, drag and drop it onto the "Attachments" field or click the field and then select a file.

10. Check the sales tax and apply a discount, shipping, and deposit, if needed:

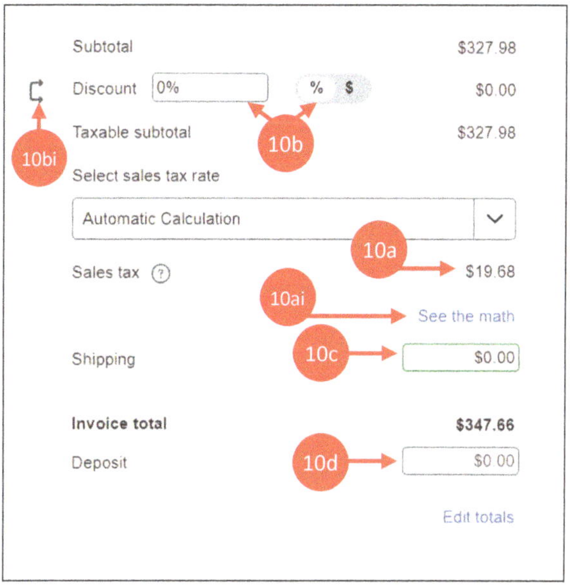

Figure 84: A picture of the totals and subtotals area in an invoice in QuickBooks Online. The numbers and letters match the steps in this activity.

   a. Check the sales tax amount.
      i. If using automatic sales tax, click the "See the math" link to check it in a pane that opens and change it, if needed.
   b. Optionally, to discount the invoice total, click the "Discount" field to change it to a percent or amount, as needed; then enter the percentage or amount.
      i. To change whether to apply it before or after calculating sales tax, click the arrows next to it.
   c. Enter the shipping amount, if needed.
   d. Optionally, to record a deposit if you enabled the "Deposit" field, enter the amount into the field and click outside it.

i. Then record the deposit details for the "Amount," "Payment method (optional)," "Reference no. (optional)" and the "Deposit to" account in the "Deposit" pane that opens.

ii. To return to the "Manage" pane after entering deposit details, click the "<" button in the pane's upper-left corner.

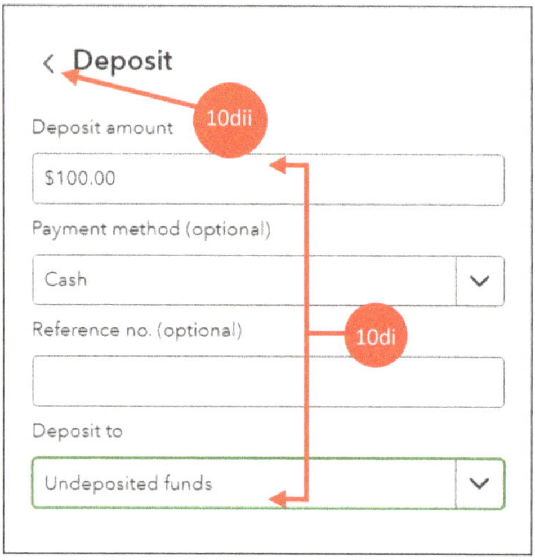

Figure 85: A picture of the "Deposit" pane that appears if you collect a deposit on an invoice in QuickBooks Online. The numbers and letters match the steps in this activity.

11. To preview the invoice, click the "Edit," "Email view," "Payor view," and "PDF view" tabs in the toolbar at the top of the invoice, as needed. "Edit" is the view you use to edit the invoice.

Figure 86: A picture of the toolbar at the top of an invoice when using the default "Modern" template in QuickBooks Online. The number matches the step in this activity.

12. Finish saving and/or sending the invoice by selecting a button in the toolbar at the bottom of the window:

Figure 87: A picture of the buttons in the toolbar at the bottom of an invoice in QuickBooks Online. The numbers and letters match the steps in this activity.

   a. To save and print or download the invoice or its packing slip, click the "Print or download" link and then select the desired command.
   b. To save it, click the "Save" button.
   c. To save it and open a new invoice or close it, click the drop-down on the "Save" button and select either "Save and new" or "Save and close."
   d. To save and send it by text or email, click the "Review and send" button.
   e. To save it and send a link to the online invoice by email, click the drop-down on the green button at the right end of the toolbar and "Share link."
      i. The link also appears in a window onscreen, so you can copy it to send via other channels, if desired.
      ii. Then close the link window.

7.2- Entering Sales Receipts in QuickBooks Online

You enter sales receipts in QuickBooks Online to record customer sales when the customer pays you at the time of sale. Some small businesses that don't track individual customer sales might also use a sales receipt to record total sales, like daily cash sales from a cash register, for example.

To create a sales receipt in QuickBooks Online:

1. Hover over the "+ Create" button in the Navigation Bar.
2. Select "Sales receipt" under "Customers."

3. Select a customer from the "Customer" drop-down.
    a. To add a new customer, select "Add new," enter their details, and save it.

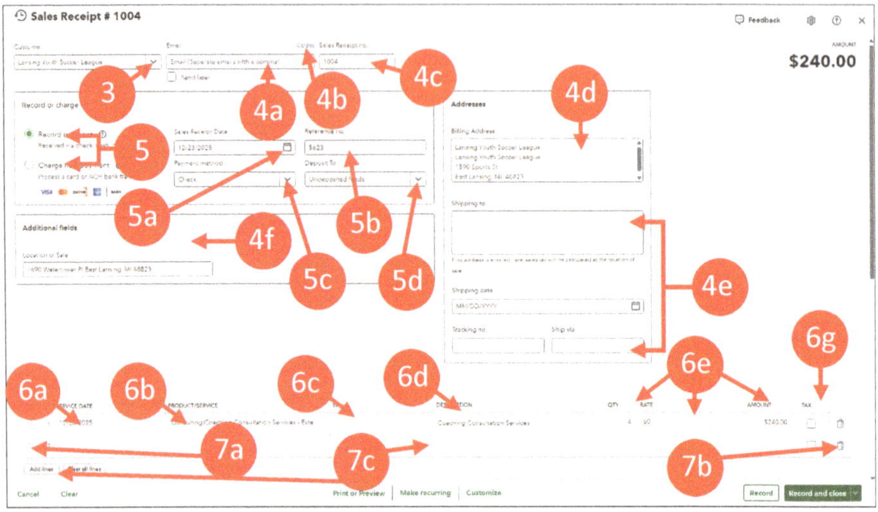

Figure 88: A picture of the "Sales Receipt" window in QuickBooks Online. The numbers and letters match steps 3 through 7 in this activity.

4. The customer's information fills in the fields at the top and right side of the form, but you can change these values, if needed.
    a. If needed, enter the customer's "Email."
    b. Optionally, to add Cc or Bcc email addresses, click the "Cc/Bcc" link, enter email addresses, and click "Done."
    c. The "Sales Receipt no" field shows the next available sales receipt number, which you can change if you enabled custom transaction numbers in sales forms.
    d. Ensure the "Billing address" field shows the customer's billing address and change it if needed.
    e. If you enabled shipping, check the "Shipping to," "Ship via," "Shipping date," and "Tracking no." field values.
    f. Optionally, in the "Additional fields" section, enter any custom fields, location, or class per transaction fields if you enabled them. The "Location of sale" field shows your company's default sales address, which you can change, if needed, and which is used for automated sales tax calculations if no customer address is entered.

5. In the "Record or Charge" section, select either the "Record payment" option to record a received payment or select "Charge new payment" to charge a new payment.
    a. Check and change the "Sales Receipt date," if needed.
    b. Optionally, enter any payment "Reference no." in the field, like a check number, for example.
    c. Use the "Payment method" drop-down to select the sales receipt's payment method.
    d. If you select the "Record payment" option, then use the "Deposit to" drop-down to select the account into which to deposit the received payment.
    e. To process an ACH or credit card payment ***after*** completing the sales receipt if you select the "Record new payment" option and select "Check" or "Credit Card" from the "Payment method" drop-down, click the "Enter bank info" or "Enter credit card details" button that appears here to open a new window.
        i. Then enter the bank or credit card details, check the save credit card or approval checkbox after getting your customer's approval, and click the "Submit" button to charge the payment.
6. Enter all the line item details for the sales receipt. Repeat this for each line item row:
    a. To select a service date, if enabled, use the "Service Date" field.
    b. To select an item from the Products and services list, use the "Product/Service" drop-down.
    c. If SKUs are enabled, check the "SKU" field's value.
    d. Check the "Description" field and change it if needed.
    e. If you enabled quantity and rate fields in sales forms, then enter the quantity and rate into the "Quantity" and "Rate" fields to calculate the amount in the "Amount" field.
        i. Alternatively, if you select a product or service without a rate or quantity or didn't enable them, then enter the total amount into the "Amount" field, if needed.

f. Optionally, to assign each item a class if you enabled classes per row, use the "Class" drop-down.

g. If the product or service is taxable, ensure the "Tax" checkbox is checked.

i. You can check or uncheck this to mark it as taxable or non-taxable.

7. To manage the line items:

a. To move a line item up or down, click and drag it by the handle at its left end.

b. To delete a line item, click the "Delete" button to its right.

c. To add a new row, either click into the bottom row or click the "Add lines" button under the rows.

8. Optionally, enter any messages or attachments:

a. To enter a message shown on the form, type it into the "Message displayed on sales receipt" field.

b. To enter a message shown for this sales receipt in the customer's statement, type it into the "Message displayed on statement" field.

c. To attach a file, drag and drop it onto the "Attachments" field or click the field and select a file.

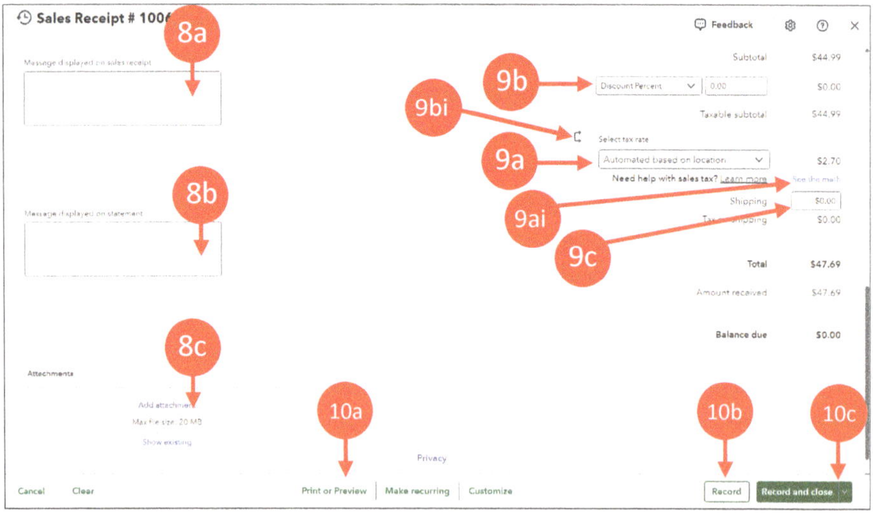

Figure 89: A picture of the "Sales Receipt" window in QuickBooks Online. The numbers and letters match steps 8 through 10 in this activity.

9. Check the sales tax and apply a discount, shipping, and deposit, if needed:
    a. Check the sales tax amount.
        i. If using automatic sales tax, click the "See the math" link to check it in a pane that opens and change it, if needed.
    b. Optionally, to discount the sales receipt total, select either the value or percent choice from the "Discount" drop-down, as needed; then enter the percentage or amount.
        i. To change whether to apply it before or after calculating sales tax, click the arrows next to it.
    c. Enter the shipping amount, if needed.
10. Finish saving and/or sending the form by selecting a button in the toolbar at the bottom of the window:
    a. To save and then print or download the sales receipt or its packing slip, or to mark it to print later, click the "Print or preview" button and then select the desired command.
    b. To record or charge it, click the "Record/Charge" button.
    c. To record or charge it and then email it, open a new sales receipt, or close it, click or select a choice from the "Record/Charge and send / Record/Charge and new / Record/Charge and close" drop-down button.

7.3- Finding Transactions in QuickBooks Online

You can easily find transactions in QuickBooks Online. This lets you quickly access a form from anywhere in the program without opening its transaction window to find it.

To find a transaction in QuickBooks Online:

1. Click the "Search" field, which contains a magnifying glass icon.
2. To open a recent transaction:
    a. Recent transactions appear in the drop-down menu.
    b. Click a transaction to open it.
3. To search for a transaction:
    a. Type your search term in the "Search" field.
    b. Matching results appear below it.
    c. Click the result to open it.

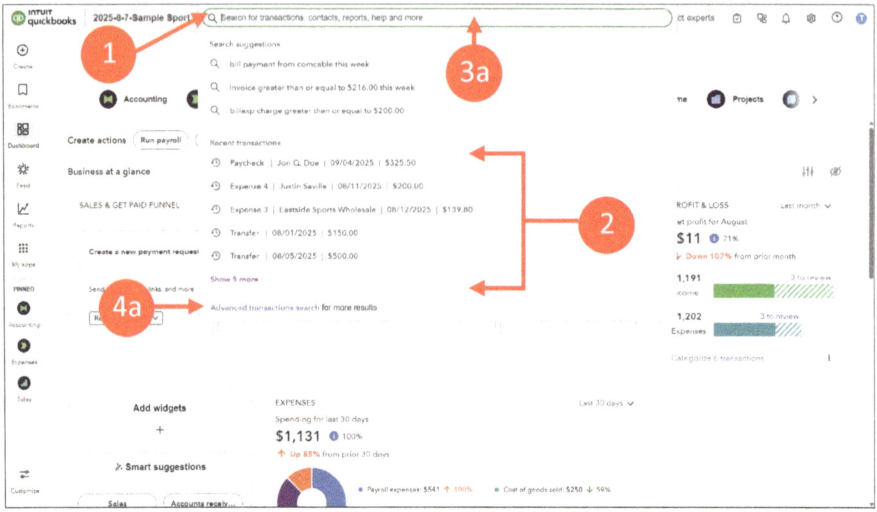

Figure 90: A picture showing the "Search" bar and menu in QuickBooks Online. The numbers and letters match the steps in this activity.

4. To do an advanced search:
    a. Click "Advanced transactions search" at the bottom of the drop-down menu.

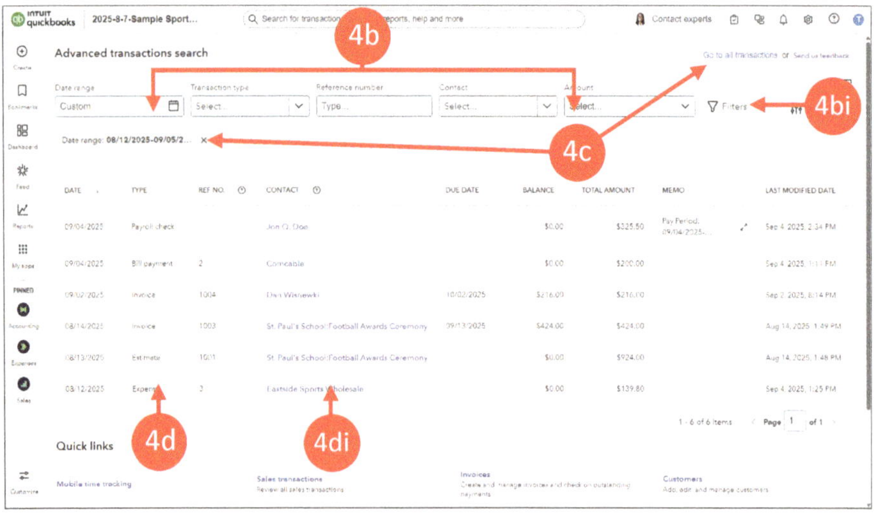

Figure 91: A picture of the "Advanced transactions search" page in QuickBooks Online. The numbers and letters match the steps in this activity.

b. In the page that opens, select the filter criteria from the fields to show matching transactions in the list below.

            i. To show more filters, click the “Filters” button to the right of the filter fields, make filtering selections, and click the “Apply” button.

    c. To clear filters, click the "X" button on an applied filter to clear it or click “Go to all transactions” to clear all filters.
    d. To open a transaction in a new window, click it.
        i. Avoid clicking its “Contact” link unless you want to view the contact’s record.

7.4- Printing Sales Forms in QuickBooks Online

How to print a sales form in QuickBooks Online:

1. Open the sales form to print.
2. To print the form:
    a. Click the “Print or Preview” button for credit memos, refund receipts, and sales receipts.
    b. Click the “Print or download” button for invoices and estimates.
    c. Click the “Print” button for received payments and sales orders.
3. A PDF preview of the sales form then opens.
    a. Right-click it and select “Print” or click the “Print” icon in its toolbar.

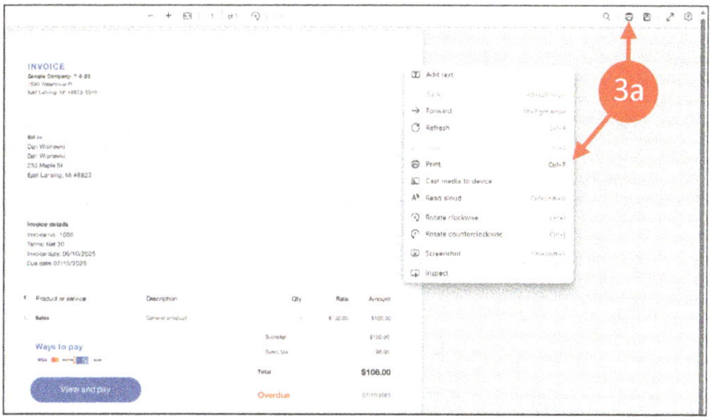

Figure 92: A picture showing how to print an invoice in QuickBooks Online from its PDF preview window. The number and letter matches the step in the preceding activity.

7.5- How to Batch Print Sales Forms in QuickBooks Online

To batch print sales forms in QuickBooks Online:

1. Select “Sales & Get Paid” then “Sales transactions” from the "All apps" bar to open the “Sales transactions” page.
2. Check the boxes next to the items to print.
3. Click the “Batch actions” button and select “Print.”

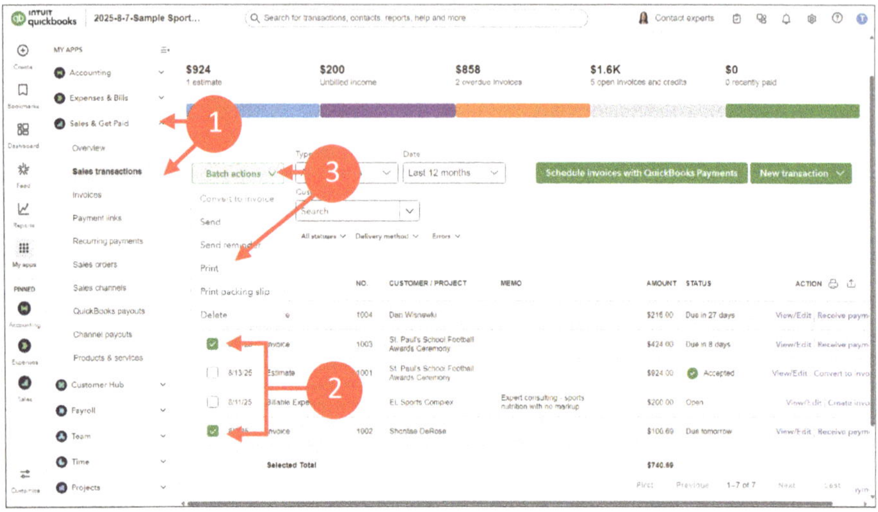

Figure 93: A picture showing how to batch print sales transactions in QuickBooks Online. The numbers match the steps in this activity.

4. A PDF preview of all the sales forms then opens.
   a. Right-click it and select “Print” or click the “Print” icon in its toolbar.
5. If asked, to mark forms as printed, click “Yes” or “No,” as needed.

7.6- Managing Sales Transactions in QuickBooks Online

The “Sales transactions” page in QuickBooks Online lets you view and manage all your sales transactions in one place.

How to view and manage sales transactions in QuickBooks Online:

1. Select “Sales & Get Paid” then “Sales transactions” from the "All apps" bar to open the “Sales transactions” page.
   a. By default, this page shows all sales for the last 365 days.
2. To filter the transactions, click a section in the Money Bar.
   a. To view all transactions, click the same section again or select “All transactions.”
3. To apply advanced filters:

   a. Use the drop-down buttons like "Type," "Date," "Customer," "Status," "Delivery method," and "Errors" to filter transactions.

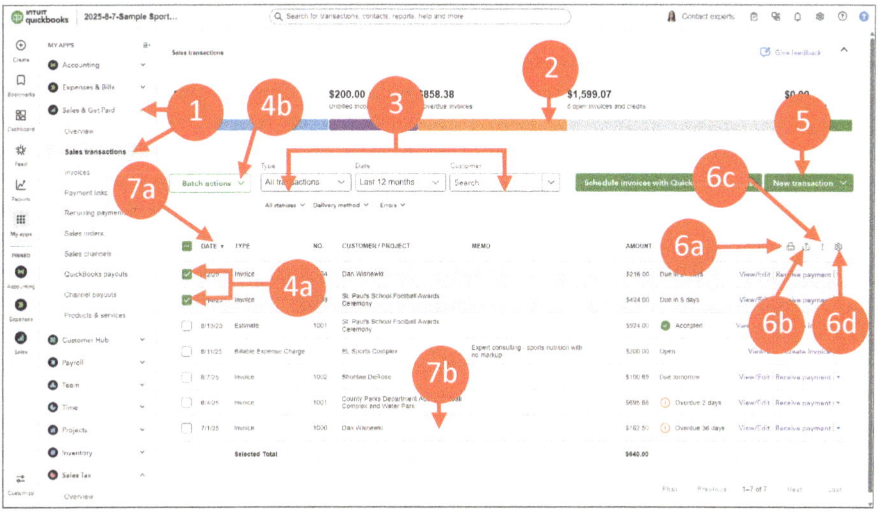

Figure 94: A picture of the "Sales transactions" page in QuickBooks Online. The numbers and letters match the steps in this activity.

4. To do batch actions on transactions:
   a. Select transactions using checkboxes.
   b. Click the "Batch actions" button and choose an action.
5. To create a new transaction, click "New transaction" and select the transaction type to create.
6. To print or export the "All Sales" transactions list, show quick links, or change list settings:
   a. To print it, click "Print list" above and to the right of the list.
   b. To export it to Excel, click "Export to Excel" above and to the right of the list.
   c. To show related activities, click "Quick links" above and to the right of the list.
   d. To show a menu of settings you can change, click "Settings" above and to the right of the list and make your changes in the menu.
7. To sort and view the transactions:
   a. To sort transactions, click the column headings in the list.

b. To show a transaction's details in a pane, click a transaction.

7.7- Creating Customer Statements in QuickBooks Online

Statements in QuickBooks Online show customer transactions based on the type of statement chosen. Businesses that bill customers often enter charges as they happen and later send a billing statement to request payment. These businesses may use "Balance Forward" or "Open Item" statements. Other businesses might use "Transaction Statements" to show the history of transactions, especially if no payment is needed.

You can enter charges for customer statements using sales forms or journal entries. The form you choose depends on whether the charges are recurring and if they are automatically paid or if the customer pays later. For recurring charges, you can create a recurring invoice, sales receipt, or journal entry. If the customer pays later, use an invoice or a journal entry with a debit to "Accounts Receivable" and a credit to the income account. For automatic or pre-payments, use a sales receipt.

If your business sends statements to remind customers of outstanding balances from normal sales and invoicing, just record your sales and invoices as usual and create the needed statements.

Before you print statements in QuickBooks Online, you should change the settings for how you want the statements to appear.

To change the statement settings in QuickBooks Online:

Figure 95: A picture of the "Statements" settings in the "Sales" settings in the "Account and Settings" window in QuickBooks Online. The numbers and letters match the steps in the following activity.

1. Click the "Settings" button in the QuickBooks Online toolbar and select "Account and settings."

2. Click "Sales" in the "Account and settings" window, then click "Statements."
    a. To show transaction details, enable the "List each transaction including all detail lines" option.
    b. To show an aging table, turn on the "Show aging table" if needed.
3. Click "Save" to save any changes.
4. Click "Done" to close.

To create customer statements in QuickBooks Online:
1. Hover over the "+ Create" button in the Navigation Bar.
2. Select "Statement" under "Customers."

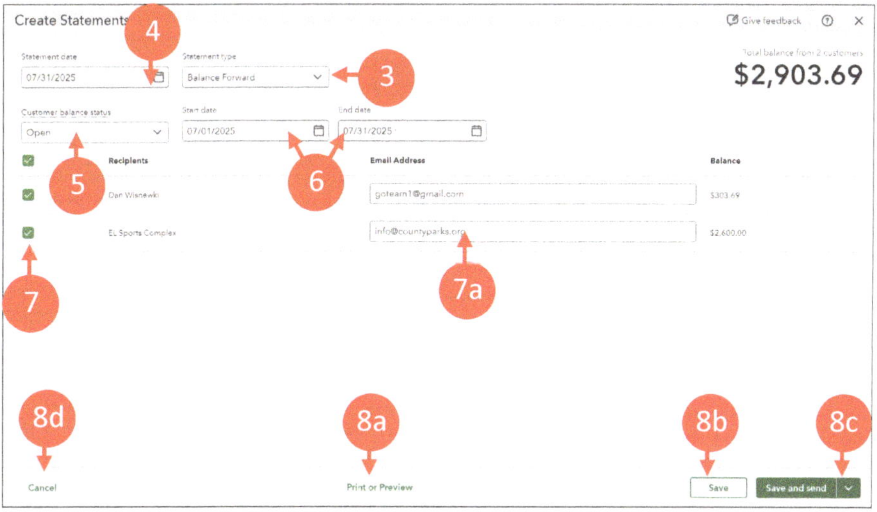

Figure 96: A picture of the "Create Statements" window in QuickBooks Online. The numbers and letters match the steps in this activity.

3. In the window that opens, choose a statement type by selecting "Balance Forward," "Open Item," or "Transaction Statement" from the "Statement type" drop-down, as needed.
4. Choose the statement date.
5. Select the customer balance status.
6. If needed, enter the start and end dates for "Balance Forward" and "Transaction Statement" types.
7. Check the boxes next to the customers to whom to send statements.
    a. Add missing email addresses if needed.

8. To save, print, email, or cancel the statements, click a toolbar button:
    a. To print or preview statements, click "Print or Preview" and then print in the PDF preview that opens.
    b. To save the statements, click "Save."
    c. To save and email statements or save and close the window, click the current choice or select a choice from the "Save and send/Save and close" drop-down button.
    d. If needed, click "Cancel" to cancel creating the statements.

CHAPTER 8- RECEIVING CUSTOMER PAYMENTS

8.1- Recording Customer Payments in QuickBooks Online

If you use QuickBooks Payments with QuickBooks Online, customer payments are automatically recorded when they pay through the link you sent. You can also manually enter payments for invoices if needed.

To manually record a customer payment in QuickBooks Online:

1. Hover over the "+ Create" button in the Navigation Bar.
2. Select "Receive payment" under "Customers" to open the Receive Payment window.

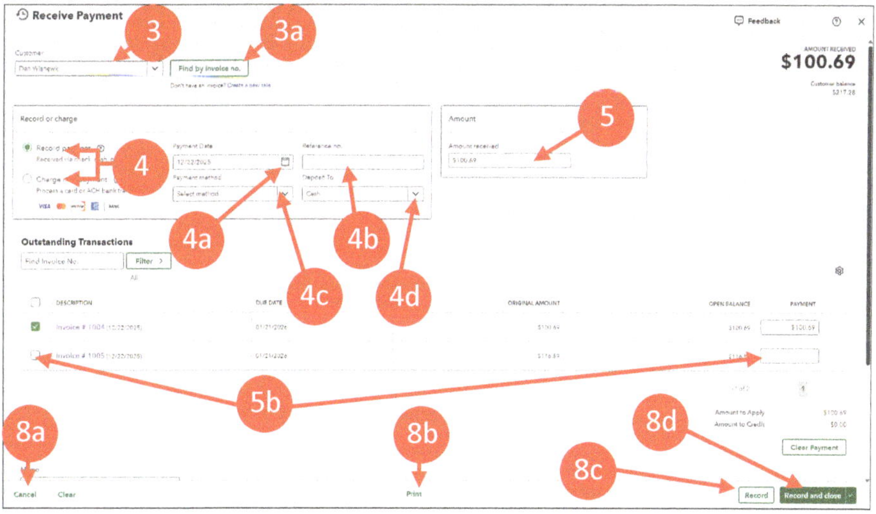

Figure 97: A picture of the "Receive Payment" window in QuickBooks Online. The numbers and letters match the steps in this activity.

3. Select the customer from the "Customer" drop-down.
    a. Alternatively, to find a customer by invoice number, click the "Find by invoice no." button, type an invoice number, and click the "Find" button.

4. In the "Record or Charge" section, select either the "Record payment" option to record a received payment or select "Charge new payment" to charge a new payment.
    a. Check and change the "Payment date," if needed.
    b. Optionally, enter any payment "Reference no." in the field, like a check number, for example.
    c. Use the "Payment method" drop-down to select the payment method.
    d. If you select the "Record payment" option, then use the "Deposit to" drop-down to select the account into which to deposit the received payment.
    e. To process an ACH or credit card payment ***after*** completing the payment's details if you select the "Record new payment" option and select "Check" or "Credit Card" from the "Payment method" drop-down, click the "Enter bank info" or "Enter credit card details" button that appears here to open a new window.
        i. Then enter the bank or credit card details, check the save credit card or approval checkbox after getting your customer's approval, and click the "Submit" button to charge the payment.
5. Enter the payment amount.
    a. QuickBooks automatically applies the payment to the oldest invoices in the "Outstanding Transactions" list.
    b. If needed, to change this, check or uncheck boxes next to invoices or change the amount to attribute to an invoice in its "Payment" column.
        i. If you do this, ensure the "Payment" total matches the "Amount received" and that you don't make any unwanted credits.
6. Optionally, enter a memo.
7. Optionally, attach files using the "Attachments" field.
8. To save, print, or cancel the payment, click a button in the toolbar:
    a. To cancel the payment, click "Cancel."
    b. To save and print the payment, click "Print" and then print from the PDF preview.

c. To record or charge the payment, click "Record/Charge."

d. To record or charge and then email, open a new payment window, or close it, select a choice from the "Record/Charge and send / Record/Charge and new / Record/Charge and close" drop-down button.

8.2- Entering Customer Overpayments

If a customer overpays an invoice, QuickBooks Online creates a customer credit. To enter an overpayment, enter the payment as usual, per the instructions in the previous lesson titled "8.1- Recording Customer Payments in QuickBooks Online." Select the customer, payment date, method, deposit account, and amount.

QuickBooks Online applies the payment to the oldest invoices first. The "Amount to Credit" field shows the overpayment amount. For example, a $150 payment against $100 of invoices shows a $50 credit. When you save the overpayment, QuickBooks Online then generates a customer credit for the overpayment amount.

8.3- Entering Customer Down Payments or Prepayments

You can easily record a customer's down payment or prepayment in QuickBooks Online. To enter an overpayment, enter the payment as usual, per the instructions in the previous lesson titled "8.1- Recording Customer Payments in QuickBooks Online." Choose the customer, enter the payment date, method, deposit account, and amount.

Ensure no items in the "Outstanding Transactions" list are checked so the entire payment is recorded as a customer credit. When you save the payment, it creates a customer credit you can apply to future invoices.

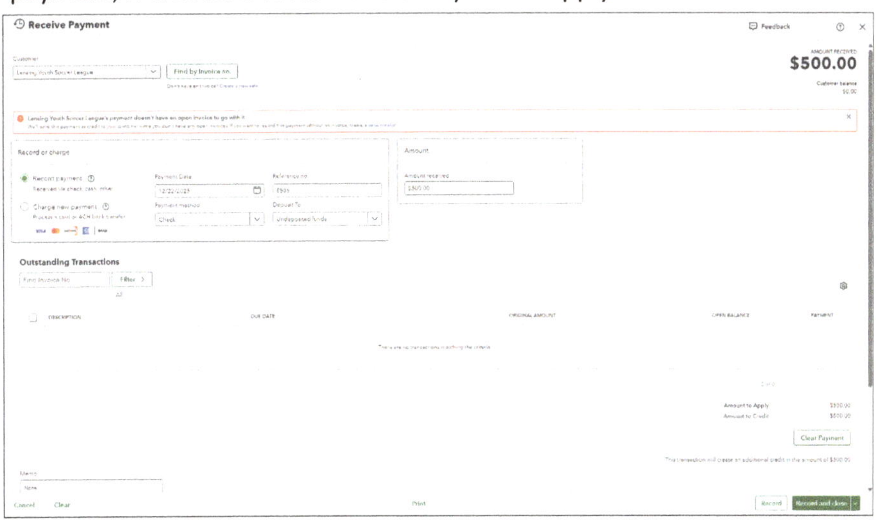

Figure 98: A picture showing a company receiving a down payment or prepayment from a customer in the "Receive Payment" window in QuickBooks Online.

8.4- Applying Customer Credits

If you turn on the "Automatically apply credits" option in the "Automation" section of the "Advanced" category in the "Account and Settings" window in QuickBooks Online, it will automatically use customer credits for their next invoice. To manually apply credits, first turn off this option in the settings.

To then manually apply a customer credit to an invoice in QuickBooks Online:

1. Hover over the "+ Create" button in the Navigation Bar.
2. Select "Receive payment" under "Customers" to open the Receive Payment window.
3. Select the customer with the outstanding invoice and credit from the "Customer" drop-down.
    a. Their invoices will appear in the "Outstanding Transactions" list.
    b. The credit will appear in the "Credits" list.
4. To apply the credit, check or uncheck the boxes next to invoices or credits to adjust their amounts, as needed, and ensure the "Payment" amounts are correct.
5. To save, print, or cancel the payment, click a button in the toolbar:
    a. To cancel the payment, click "Cancel."
    b. To save and print the payment, click "Print" and then print from the PDF preview.
    c. To record or charge the payment, click "Record/Charge."

d. To record or charge and then email, open a new payment window, or close it, select a choice from the "Record/Charge and send / Record/Charge and new / Record/Charge and close" drop-down button.

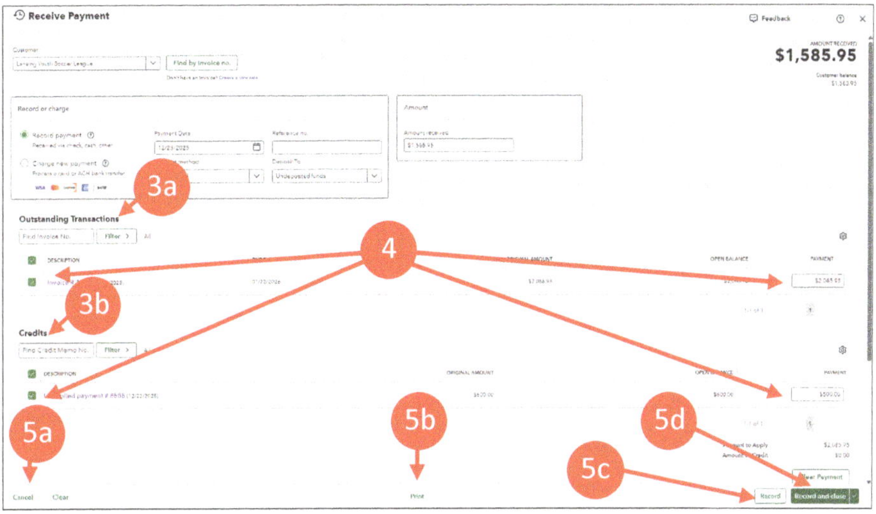

Figure 99: A picture showing how to manually apply a customer credit in the "Receive Payments" window in QuickBooks Online. The numbers and letters match the steps in the preceding activity.

Later, if it turns out the credit won't be used, you can create a credit memo and issue a refund check to refund the credit.

8.5- Recording a Bank Deposit

When you manually receive customer payments in QuickBooks Online, you use the "Deposit to" drop-down to choose the deposit account for the funds. Payments are often deposited into a "Payments to deposit" or "Undeposited Funds" account. You can then manually record a bank deposit for these funds into a bank account, like your company's checking or savings account.

How to manually record a bank deposit in QuickBooks Online:

1. Hover over the "+ Create" button in the Navigation Bar.
2. Select "Bank deposit" under "Other" to open the "Bank Deposit" window.
3. Choose the bank account into which to deposit from the "Account" drop-down.

4. Enter the deposit date.

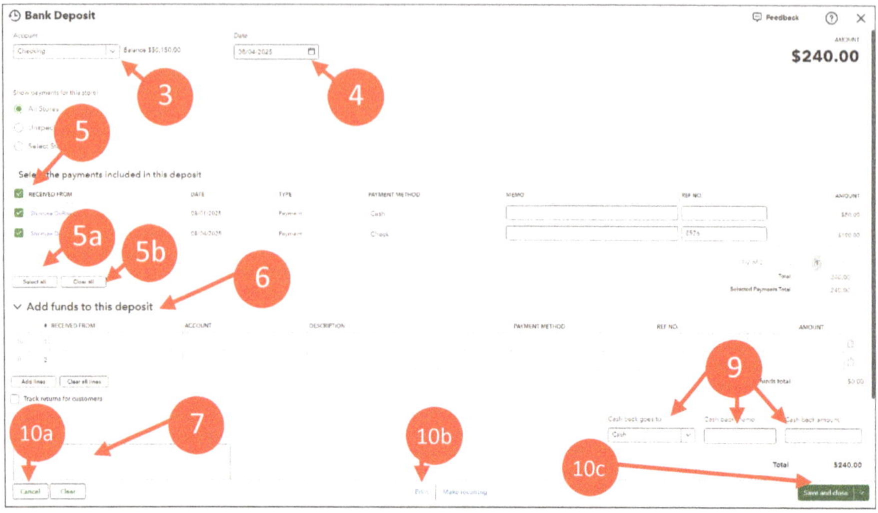

Figure 100: A picture of the "Bank Deposit" window in QuickBooks Online. The numbers and letters match the steps in this activity.

5. Check the boxes next to the payments to deposit in the list.
    a. Click "Select all" to mark all items.
    b. Click "Clear all" to unmark all items.
6. If needed, use the "Add funds to this deposit" section to add extra funds to deposit.
    a. Enter details like "Received From," "Account," "Description," and "Amount."
7. Optionally, type a note in the "Memo" field.
8. Optionally, attach files.
9. Optionally, to hold cash back, select the account for cash back in the "Cash back goes to" drop-down and enter the reason and amount for cash back.
10. To save and/or print the deposit or cancel, click a button in the toolbar:
    a. To cancel the deposit, click the "Cancel" button.
    b. To save it and print a deposit slip and summary or summary only, click the "Print" button and select either "Print deposit slip and summary" or "Print deposit summary only," as desired

c. To save it and then create a new deposit or close it, click the current choice or select the alternate choice from the "Save and new / Save and close" drop-down button.

CHAPTER 9- ENTERING CUSTOMER REFUNDS

9.1- Learn about the Different Ways to Refund Customers in QuickBooks Online

There are many ways to process customer refunds in QuickBooks Online. If a customer wants a credit for a return or refund, you can create a credit memo or a delayed credit. A credit memo is a separate transaction applied to a customer's open balance, while a delayed credit is a line item credit you manually apply to future invoices.

To change whether QuickBooks automatically applies customer credits, toggle the "Automatically apply credits" option in the "Automation" section of the "Advanced" settings.

For immediate refunds via cash, check, or credit card, create a refund receipt. If a customer wants a refund for a down payment or prepayment, write them a check or expense and match it to the existing credit.

You and the customer can decide the best option for your situation.

9.2- Creating a Credit Memo in QuickBooks Online

You can create a credit memo in QuickBooks Online if a customer wants a credit for a refund or return. The credit memo is a separate transaction you can apply to a customer's open balance.

How to create a credit memo in QuickBooks Online:

1. Hover over the "+ Create" button in the Navigation Bar.
2. Select "Credit memo" under "Customers" to open the "Credit Memo" window.
3. Choose a customer from the "Customer" drop-down.
    a. Add their email if needed.
    b. To add cc or bcc emails, click "Cc/Bcc," enter emails, click "Done."
4. To send the credit memo later, check the "Send later" checkbox.
5. Select the date from the "Credit Memo Date" field.
6. The credit memo's number appears in the "Credit Memo no." field, and you can change it if you enabled custom transaction numbers.

7. Optionally, if you enabled classes per transaction or locations, use the “Class” and “Location” drop-downs to select choices.
8. To select the credited items and enter refund information, select choices from the “Product/Service” column.
9. Alternatively, to create a new general “Credit” line item, select the “+Add new” choice from the “Product/Service” drop-down and create it in the product/service information pane that then appears.
    a. If you do this, use care to select the correct income account and set its correct taxable setting.
10. The “Total Credit” towards the lower-right corner of the window shows the total credit amount.
11. To save and/or send it or print it, click a button in the toolbar:
    a. To save and print it, click the “Print or Preview” command.
    b. To save it and then send it, create a new credit memo, or close it, click the current choice or select an alternate choice from the “Save and send” drop-down button.

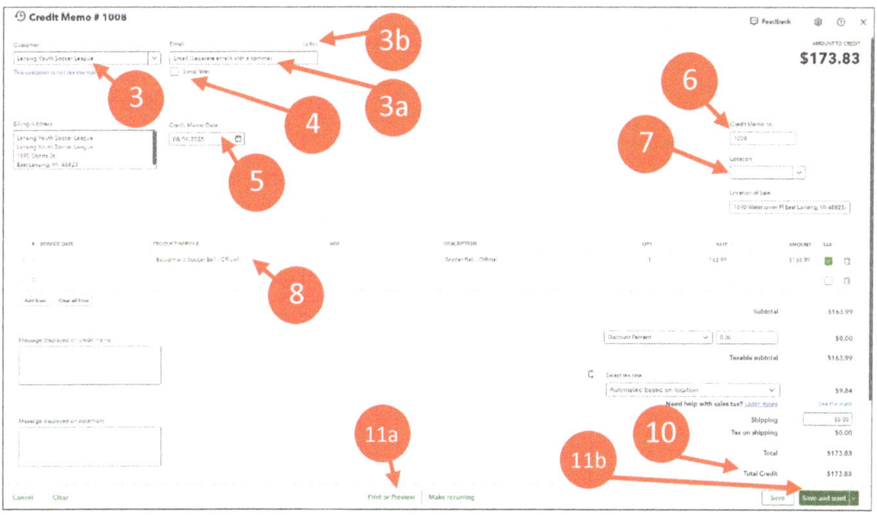

Figure 101: A picture of the "Credit Memo" window in QuickBooks Online. The numbers and letters match the steps in the preceding activity.

9.3- Creating a Refund Receipt in QuickBooks Online

If a customer wants a refund in the form of a check, cash, or credit card, you can create a refund receipt instead of a credit memo. A refund receipt gives the customer cash, a check, or a credit card refund instead of a credit to their balance or future invoices.

How to create a refund receipt in QuickBooks Online:

1. Hover over the "+ Create" button in the Navigation Bar.
2. Select "Refund receipt" under "Customers" to open the "Refund Receipt" window.

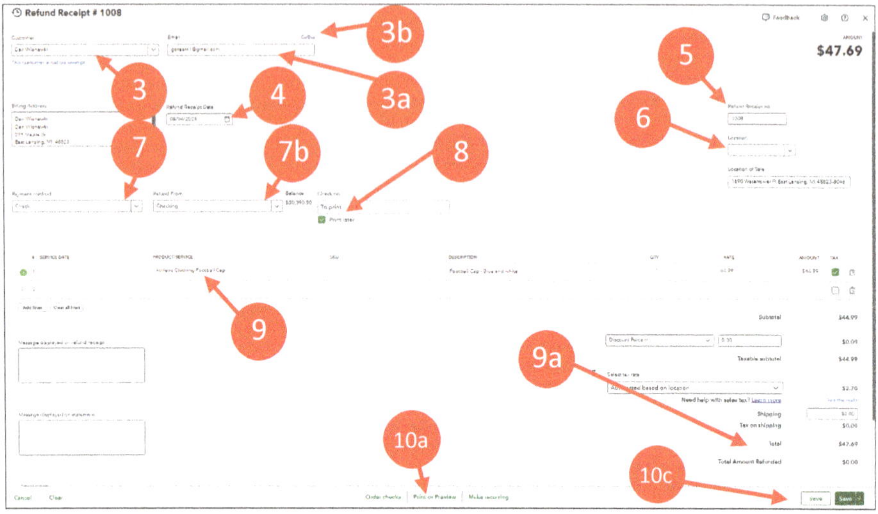

Figure 102: A picture of the "Refund Receipt" window in QuickBooks Online. The numbers and letters match the steps in this activity.

3. Choose a customer from the "Customer" drop-down.
    a. Add their email if needed.
    b. To add cc or bcc emails, click "Cc/Bcc," enter emails, click "Done."
4. Select the date from the "Refund Receipt date" field.
5. The refund receipt's number appears in the "Refund Receipt no." field, and you can change it if you enabled custom transaction numbers.
6. Optionally, if you enabled classes per transaction or locations, use the "Class" and "Location" drop-downs to select choices.
7. Choose the payment method from the "Payment method" drop-down.
    a. For credit card refunds, enter the credit card information.
    b. For cash or check refunds, select the account from the "Refund From" drop-down.
8. If refunding by check, enter the check number or check "Print later" if you want to print the check later.

9. To select the refunded items and enter refund information, select choices from the "Product/Service" column.
    a. Ensure the refund "Amount" is correct.
10. To finish, click a button in the toolbar:
    a. To refund by check, click "Print or Preview" and then click "Print check" to save the refund receipt and print the check
    b. For credit card refunds, the amount is refunded immediately or during batch processing.
    c. If returning a cash refund or after completing the other options, click or select a save choice by using the "Save" buttons.

9.4- Refunding Customer Payments by Check in QuickBooks Online

If a customer makes a customer payment as a prepayment or down payment for a future order in QuickBooks Online and then cancels the order, you can give a refund using a check. This lets you remove the customer credit. You can also use the "Expense" window instead of the "Check" window if you prefer or if the refund was cash.

To refund a customer prepayment or down payment by check:

1. Hover over the "+ Create" button in the Navigation Bar.
2. Select "Check" under the "Vendors" heading.

Figure 103: A picture of a customer refund check in QuickBooks Online. The numbers and letters match the steps in this activity.

3. Choose the customer's name from the "Payee" drop-down.
4. Select the bank account from the "Bank Account" drop-down.

5. Enter the payment date in the “Payment Date” field.
6. To print the check later, check the “Print later” checkbox.
    a. Otherwise, enter the check number in the “Check no.” field.
7. In the “Category details” list, select “Accounts Receivable (A/R)” or the specific accounts receivable account used for the initial payment.
8. Optionally, enter a description for the refund in the “Description” column.
9. Enter the refund amount in the “Amount” column.
10. Click the “Print check” button to print the check, or select a save option from the “Save and close” drop-down button.

To manually apply the refund to the customer credit:

1. Hover over the “+ Create” button in the Navigation Bar.
2. Select “Receive payment” from the menu.

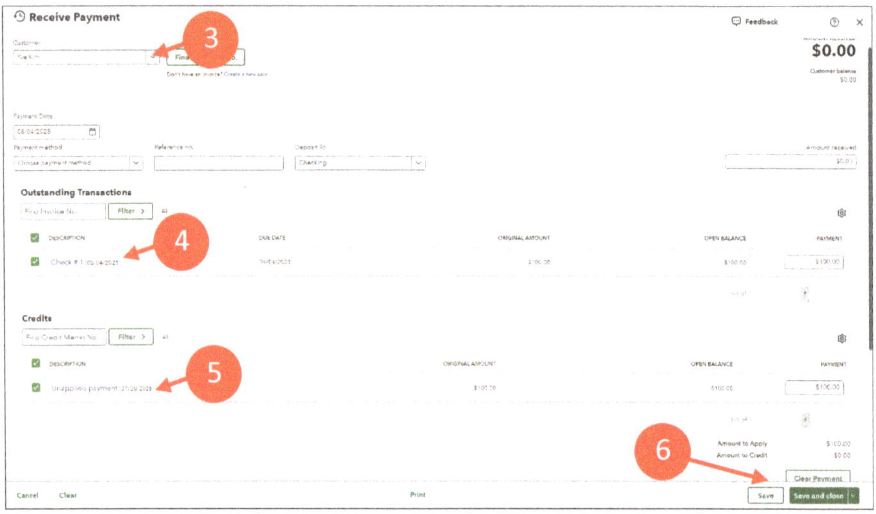

Figure 104: A picture showing how to manually apply a refund check to an existing customer credit in QuickBooks Online. The numbers and letters match the steps in this activity.

3. Choose the refunded customer's name from the “Customer” drop-down.
4. Ensure the check or expense you created appears and is selected in the “Outstanding Transactions” list.

5. Ensure the existing customer credit appears and is selected in the "Credits" list.
6. Click or select a save option from the "Save" buttons to finish and save the payment.

9.5- Creating a Delayed Credit in QuickBooks Online

A delayed credit in QuickBooks Online is a way to create customer credits you can use in future invoices. These credits are not used until you manually add them to an invoice.

How to create a delayed credit in QuickBooks Online:

1. Hover over the "+ Create" button in the Navigation Bar.
2. Select "Delayed credit" under "Customers."

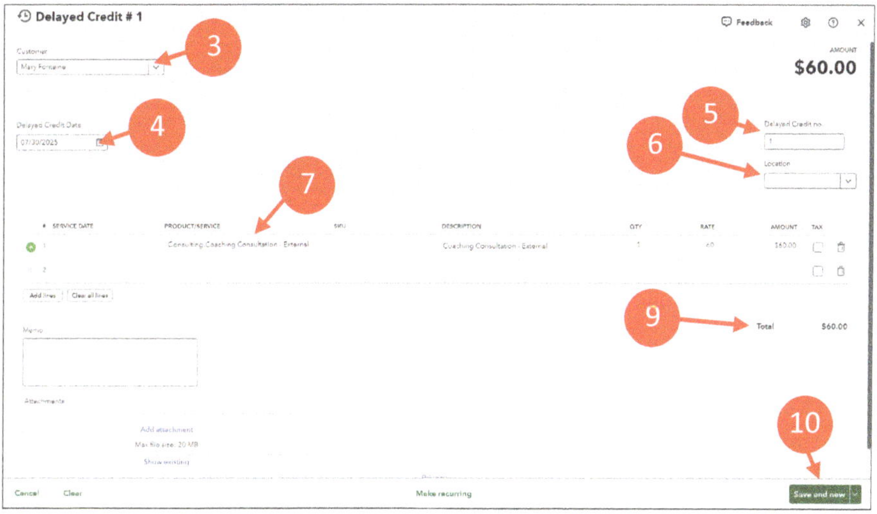

Figure 105: A picture of the "Delayed Credit" window in QuickBooks Online. The numbers match the steps in this activity.

3. Choose the customer's name from the "Customer" drop-down.
4. Enter the creation date in the "Delayed Credit date" field.
5. If needed, change the "Delayed Credit" number.
6. Select the "Class" and "Location," if applicable.
7. In the "Product/Service" column, select the products or services for the credit and enter the refund details.
8. To create a new general "Credit" line item, select +Add new from the Product/Service drop-down.
9. Make sure the total amount to credit is correct.
10. Save the delayed credit by selecting "Save and new" or "Save and close."

How to apply a delayed credit to a future invoice:

1. Open a new "Invoice" window.

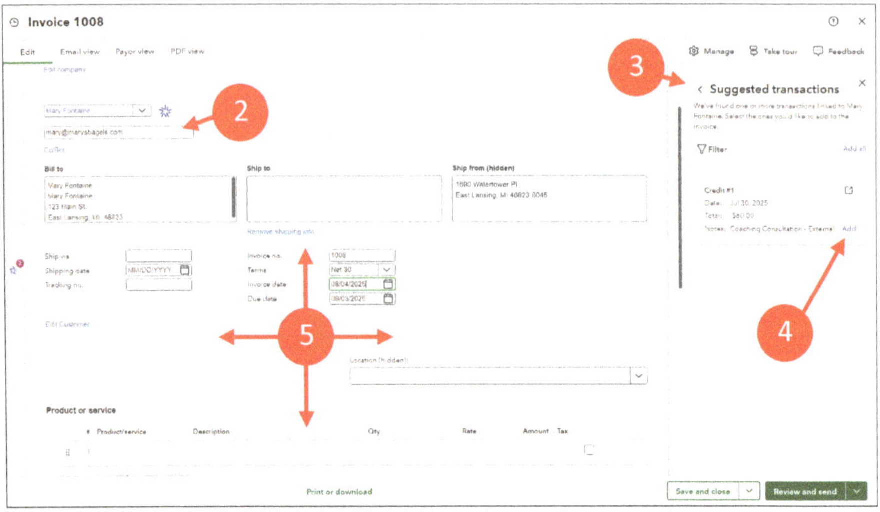

Figure 106: A picture showing how to add a delayed credit to an invoice in QuickBooks Online. The numbers match the steps in this activity.

2. Select the customer's name from the "Customer" drop-down.
3. In the "Suggested transactions" pane, find the delayed credit.
4. Click "Add" next to the credit to include it in the invoice.
5. Complete and save the invoice.

CHAPTER 10- ENTERING AND PAYING BILLS

10.1- Entering Bills in QuickBooks Online

Entering bills in QuickBooks Online lets you easily manage and pay them later. Entering and paying bills in QuickBooks Online also lets you record all the related payables information for the company's financial reports.

To enter bills in QuickBooks Online:

1. Hover over the "+ Create" button in the Navigation Bar.
2. Select "Bill" under "Vendors."

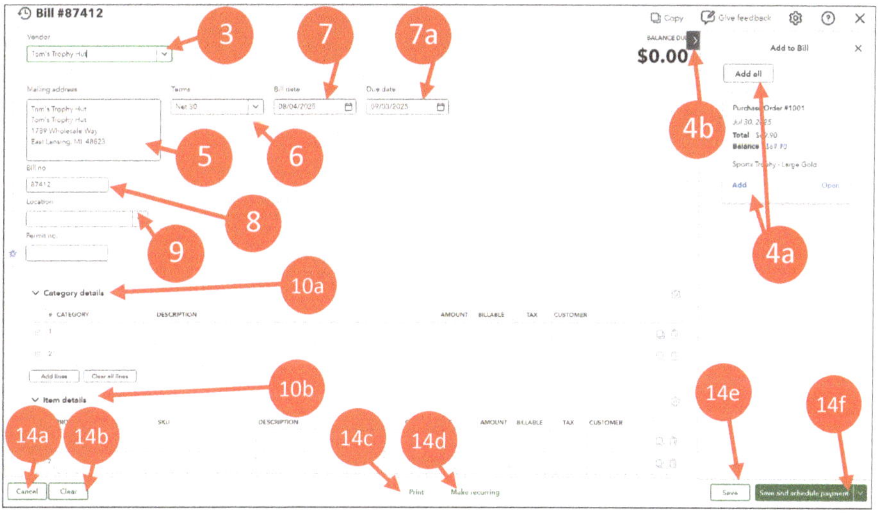

Figure 107: A picture of the "Bill" window and "Add to Bill" pane that shows any open purchase orders for the selected vendor in QuickBooks Online. The numbers and letters match the steps in this activity.

3. Choose the vendor from the drop-down menu.
    a. If the vendor is new, click "+ Add new" and enter their details.
4. Enter the bill details:
    a. If there are purchase orders, click "Add" or "Add all" in the "Add to Bill" pane that appears to include them.

   b. If you don't want to add purchase orders, click the arrow to collapse the pane.
5. Check the vendor's mailing address.
   a. Type it in if it's missing.
6. Select payment terms from the "Terms" drop-down.
   a. You can add new terms if needed.
7. Enter the bill date.
   a. The due date will adjust automatically.
8. Enter the bill number.
9. Select a location if needed.
10. Enter line item details:
    a. For bills not related to products/services, use the "Category details" section.
    b. For bills related to products/services, use the "Item details" section.
11. Delete or add lines as needed.
12. Type a memo if you want to add notes.
13. Attach files if needed.
14. Manage the bill using the toolbar:
    a. Click "Cancel" to cancel.
    b. Click "Clear" to clear all entries.
    c. Click "Print" to save and print.
    d. Click "Make recurring" to set up recurring bills.
    e. Click "Save" to save the bill.
    f. Use the “Save and new / Save and close / Save and schedule payment” drop-down button to save and open a new bill, close the window, or schedule a payment.

10.2- Paying Bills in QuickBooks Online

Paying the bills you enter into QuickBooks Online helps you manage the company’s payables and record its expenses for financial reports.

To pay bills in QuickBooks Online:

1. Hover over the “+ Create” button in the Navigation Bar.
2. Select "Pay bills" under "Vendors."
3. Choose the payment account from the drop-down menu.
4. Enter the payment date.
5. Decide if you want to print bill payment checks later:
   a. If “Yes,” then check the "Print later" box.

b. If "No," uncheck it and enter the starting check number you used.

Figure 108: A picture of the "Pay Bills" window in QuickBooks Online. The numbers and letters match the steps in this activity.

6. To filter the bills, if needed:
   a. Click "Filters" and choose your options.
   b. Click "Apply" to set the filter.
   c. Click "Reset" to remove filters.
7. Select the bills to pay:
   a. Check the box next to each bill.
   b. Check the top box to select all bills.
8. Enter payment amounts:
   a. Full payment amount appears automatically.
   b. Enter a smaller amount for partial payments.
9. Manage the payments using the toolbar:
   a. If needed, click "Cancel" to cancel.
   b. Otherwise, click or select a choice from the drop-down button at the right end of the toolbar to select a save option:
      i. Click "Save" to save.
      ii. Click "Save and print" to print checks.
      iii. Click "Save and close" to save and close.

iv. Click "Schedule payment(s)" to schedule online payments.

10.3- Entering a Vendor Credit in QuickBooks Online

You can enter a vendor credit in QuickBooks Online to return an item to a vendor or enter a credit for overpaying an earlier bill.

How to create a vendor credit in QuickBooks Online:

1. Hover over the "+ Create" button in the Navigation Bar.
2. Select "Vendor credit" under "Vendors."

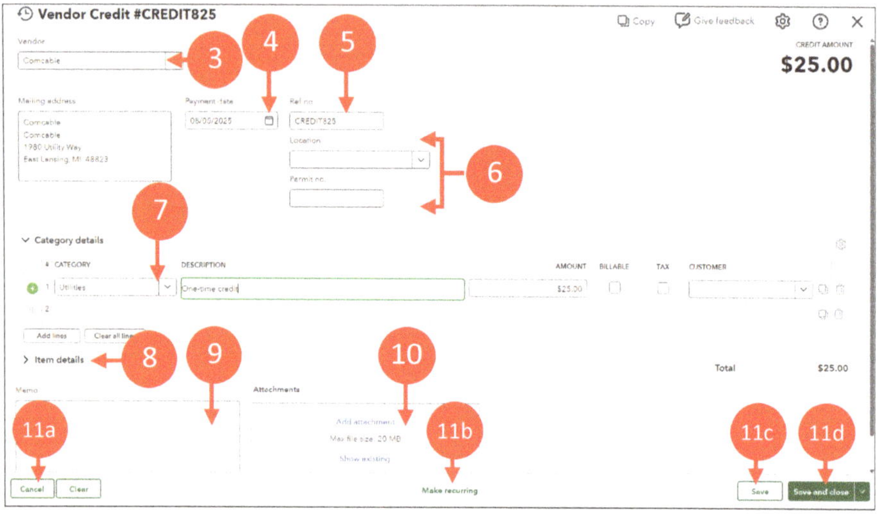

Figure 109: A picture of the "Vendor Credit" window in QuickBooks Online. The numbers and letters match the steps in this activity.

3. Choose the vendor from the drop-down menu.
4. Enter the credit date.
5. Enter a reference number if needed.
6. If needed, fill out the remaining fields.
7. If not returning items, choose the account to which to apply the credit in "Category details" and fill in the credit info.
8. If returning items, select items to return in "Item details."
9. Add a note in the "Memo" field, if needed.
10. Attach a file, if needed.
11. Manage the vendor credit using the toolbar:
    a. Click "Cancel" to cancel.
    b. Click "Make recurring" to set up recurring credits.
    c. Click "Save" to save the vendor credit.

d. Click the button or select a choice from the green "Save and close/Save and new" drop-down button to save it and then either close the window or open a new window.

10.4- Applying a Vendor Credit in QuickBooks Online

After you enter a vendor credit in QuickBooks Online, you can then apply the vendor credit to the next bill payment to the vendor.

To apply a vendor credit to a bill payment in QuickBooks Online:

1. Hover over the “+ Create” button in the Navigation Bar.
2. Select "Pay bills" under "Vendors."

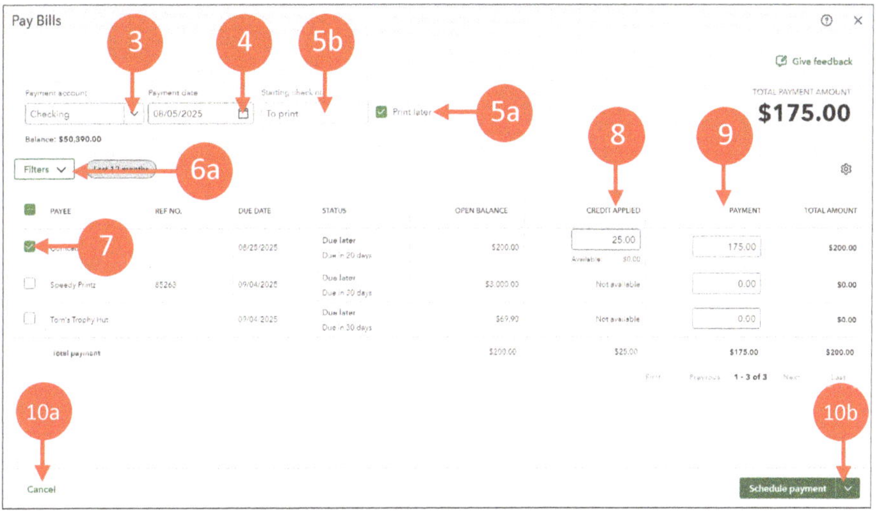

Figure 110: A picture showing how to apply a vendor credit in the "Pay Bills" window in QuickBooks Online. The numbers and letters match the steps in this activity.

3. Choose the payment account from the drop-down menu.
4. Enter the payment date.
5. Decide if you want to print the bill payment check later:
    a. If “Yes,” then check the "Print later" box.
    b. If “No,” uncheck it and enter the check number you used.
6. Find the bill:
    a. Scroll through the list or use "Filters."
7. Check the box next to the bill to apply the vendor credit.
8. Adjust the credit amount in the "Credit Applied" column if needed.
9. Check the payment amount in the "Payment" field.
10. Manage the payment using the toolbar:
    a. If needed, click "Cancel" to cancel.

b. Otherwise, click or select a choice from the drop-down button at the right end of the toolbar to select a save option:
    i. Click "Save" to save.
    ii. Click "Save and print" to print checks.
    iii. Click "Save and close" to save and close.
    iv. Click "Schedule payment(s)" to schedule online payments.

CHAPTER 11- HOW TO USE BANK ACCOUNTS

11.1- Using Account Registers in QuickBooks Online

QuickBooks Online Plus lets you add, change, and delete transactions in account registers for balance sheet accounts. You can't do this for "Accounts Payable," "Accounts Receivable," and some "Equity" accounts. For these, you need to use the associated forms. But for most other balance sheet accounts, you can use the registers like a paper checkbook.

To use account registers in QuickBooks Online:

1. Click the "Settings" button in the QuickBooks Online toolbar.
2. Select "Chart of accounts" under "Your Company."
3. Click "View Register" in the "Action" column next to the account to view the account's "Register" page.

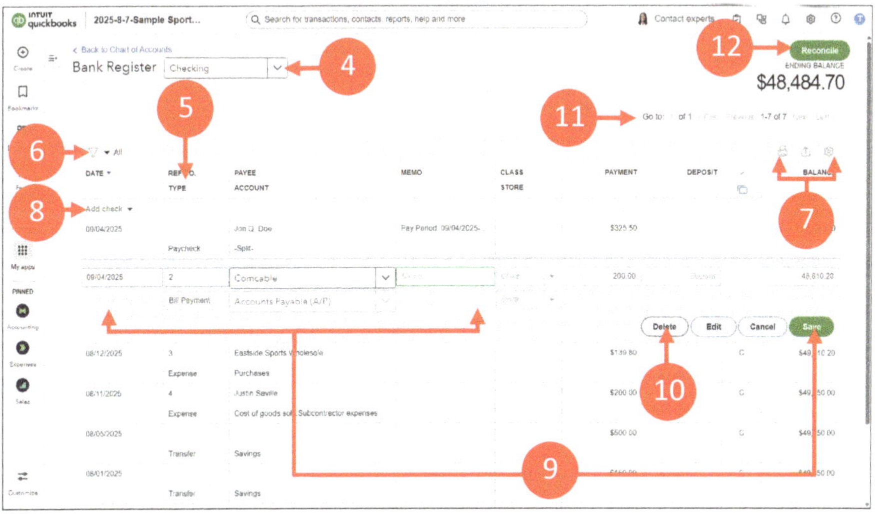

Figure 111: A picture of the "Bank Register" window for a selected "Checking" account in QuickBooks Online. The numbers match the steps in this activity.

4. To switch accounts, use the drop-down at the top of the page.
5. To sort transactions, click the column headings.
6. To filter transactions, select choices from the "Filter" button.

7. Print, export, or change settings using buttons in the upper-right corner of the list of transactions.
8. To add a new transaction, click the "Add (transaction type)" link or select a transaction type from its drop-down, enter the transaction's details, and click "Save."
9. To edit a transaction, click it, change the values in its fields, and click "Save."
10. To delete a transaction, click it, click "Delete," then confirm the deletion.
11. To scroll through pages if there are multiple pages of transactions, click the links in the "Go to:" section at either the top or bottom of the page (depending on settings).
12. To reconcile the account, click the "Reconcile" button.

11.2- Writing Checks in QuickBooks Online

QuickBooks Online lets you write checks you can print or simply record to note withdrawals from bank accounts.

To write a check in QuickBooks Online:

1. Hover over the "+ Create" button in the Navigation Bar.
2. Select "Check" under "Vendors."

Figure 112: A picture of the "Check" window in QuickBooks Online. The numbers and letters match the steps in this activity.

3. Choose the payee from the drop-down menu.
   a. To add a new payee, if needed, select "+ Add new" from the drop-down and then select the type of contact to

create and fill-in their fields in the pane that opens at the right side of the screen.

4. Select the bank account from which to withdraw funds.
5. Enter the payment date.
6. Decide if you want to print the check later:
   a. If "Yes," then check the "Print later" box.
   b. If "No," uncheck it and enter the check number you used.
7. Enter the check details into the correct section:
   a. Use "Category details" to record expenses.
   b. Use "Item details" to buy products/services.
8. Add or delete line items in either section, as needed.
9. Type a memo if needed.
10. Attach files if needed.
11. Manage the check using the links in the toolbar:
    a. Click "Cancel" to cancel.
    b. Click "Clear" to clear the check.
    c. Click "Print check" to print.
    d. Click "Order checks" to buy checks.
    e. Click "Make recurring" for regular checks.
    f. Click "More" for other options like voiding or deleting.
    g. Click "Save" to save the check.
    h. Click the button or select a choice from the green "Save and close/Save and new" drop-down button to save it and then either close the window or open a new window.

11.3- Printing Checks in QuickBooks Online

You can batch print the checks you create and save in QuickBooks Online if you select the "Print later" checkbox when creating and saving the checks.

To batch print checks in QuickBooks Online:

1. Hover over the "+ Create" button in the Navigation Bar.
2. Select "Print checks" under "Vendors."
3. If it's your first time printing checks, follow the steps in the "Print checks setup" screen that then opens:
   a. Choose a check type.
   b. Print a sample check.
   c. Adjust the check alignment, if needed.
4. In the "Print Checks" window that opens, select the account with checks to print.

5. Enter the starting check number.
6. Select the checks to print by checking their checkboxes.
7. Click "Preview and print" to print or download the checks.

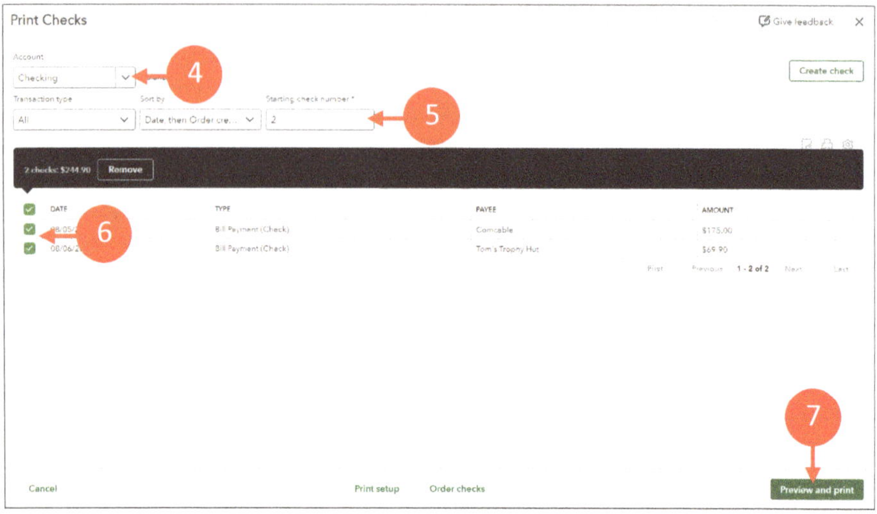

Figure 113: A picture of the "Print Checks" window in QuickBooks Online. The numbers match the steps in this activity.

8. Confirm if checks printed correctly:
    a. Select "Yes" if all printed correctly.
    b. Select "Some checks need reprinting" if some need reprinting.
    c. Select "No, keep all checks in the Print Checks list" if none printed correctly.

11.4- Transferring Funds Between Accounts in QuickBooks Online

You can record a funds transfer between two bank accounts in QuickBooks Online. Note this doesn't actually create a funds transfer between accounts at your bank. However, you can match the QuickBooks record to the actual fund transfer if you later import bank records.

To record a funds transfer in QuickBooks Online:

1. Hover over the "+ Create" button in the Navigation Bar.
2. Select "Transfer" under "Other."
3. Choose the account to transfer from using the "Transfer Funds From" drop-down.
4. Choose the account to which to transfer the funds using the "Transfer Funds To" drop-down.
5. Enter the transfer amount.

6. Enter the transfer date.
7. Add a note if needed.
8. Attach files if needed.
9. Manage the transfer using the toolbar:
    a. Click "Cancel" to cancel.
    b. Click "Clear" to clear the info.
    c. Click "Make recurring" to create regular transfers.
    d. To save it and close the window or open a new window, click or select a choice from the “Save and new / Save and close” drop-down button.

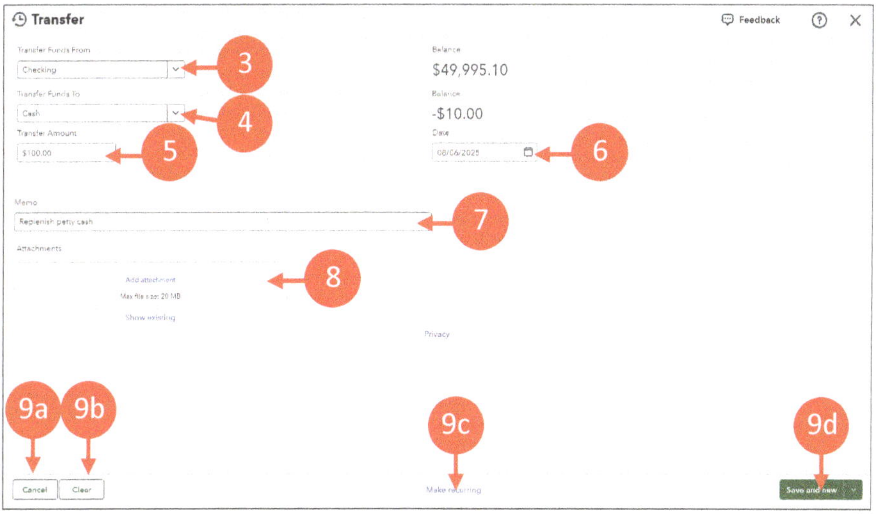

Figure 114: A picture of the "Transfer" window in QuickBooks Online. The numbers and letters match the steps in the preceding activity.

11.5- Voiding Checks in QuickBooks Online

You can void a check in QuickBooks Online to cancel the check but keep a record of it to help with account reconciliation and accurate financial accounting.

To void a check in QuickBooks Online:

1. Find and open the check you want to void.
2. Click the "More" button at the bottom.
3. Select "Void" from the pop-up menu.
4. Click "Void transaction" in the confirmation window.

11.6- Reconciling an Account in QuickBooks Online

Reconciling accounts means matching transactions from your bank statement to transactions in QuickBooks Online. You can only reconcile balance sheet accounts. If you correctly enter the account info and match all the account's transactions, the difference between the bank statement and QuickBooks should be zero. If not zero, this helps you find either bank errors or data entry errors in QuickBooks Online.

To reconcile an account in QuickBooks Online:

1. Click the "Settings" button in the QuickBooks Online toolbar.
2. Select "Reconcile" under "Tools."
3. If it's your first time reconciling, click the "Get started" and then the "Let's get reconciled" buttons.

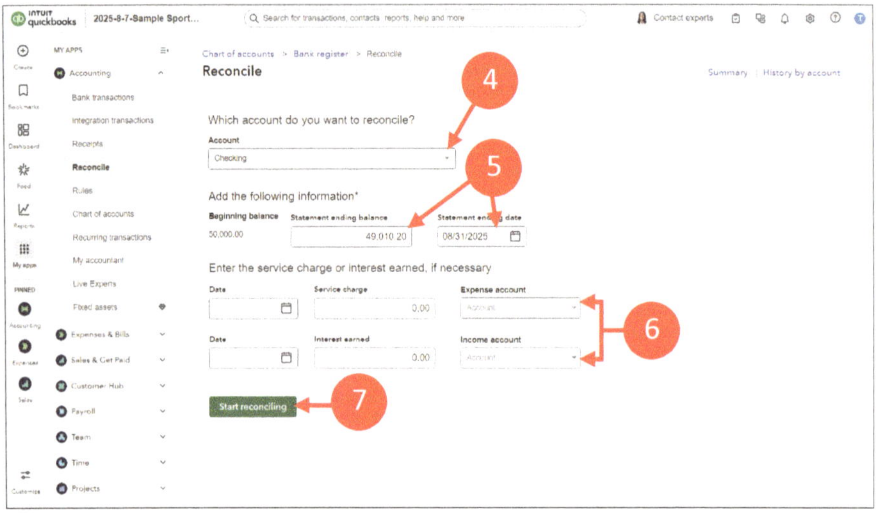

Figure 115: A picture of the initial "Reconcile" page in QuickBooks Online. The numbers match steps 4 through 7 in this activity.

4. In the initial "Reconcile" page, choose the account to reconcile from the drop-down.
5. Enter the statement's ending balance and date.
6. Add any bank fees or interest earned if needed.
7. Click "Start reconciling."
8. In the second "Reconcile" page that then opens, mark transactions as cleared by clicking the circles next to them.
9. After selecting all cleared transactions, ensure the "Difference" shown is zero.
10. If needed, to apply filters, click the "Filter" button, select choices, and click "Apply."
11. If needed, to remove filters, click the "X" to the left of an applied filter or click the "Clear filter / View all" link.
12. If needed, to edit the initial statement info you entered, click "Edit info," make the changes, and click "Save."

13. If needed, to save your work so you can finish later or investigate an account discrepancy, select "Save for later" from the drop-down button in the upper-right corner.
    a. To return later, click "Settings," then click "Reconcile" under "Tools" again.
    b. Then select the same account again and click "Resume reconciling."
14. When the difference is zero, select "Finish now" from the drop-down button in the upper-right corner to save and close.

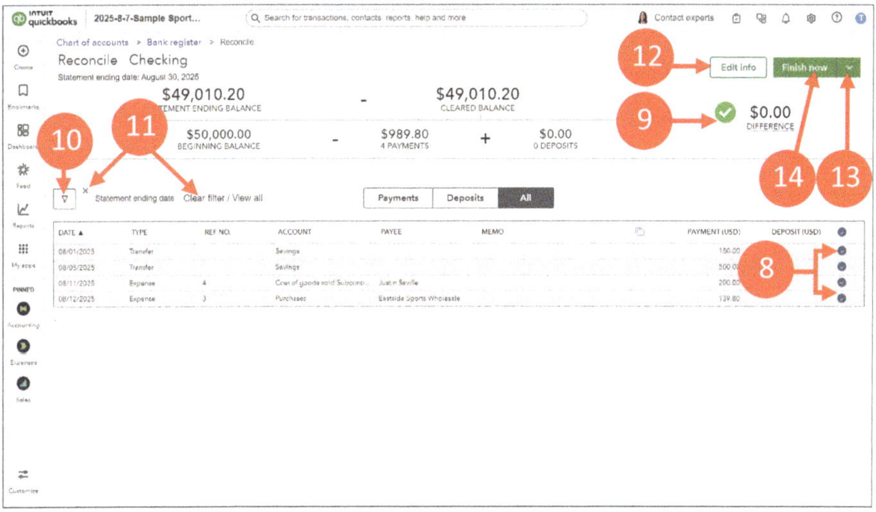

Figure 116: A picture of the second "Reconcile" window in QuickBooks Online. The numbers match steps 8 through 14 in this activity.

15. If needed, to view a reconciliation report after finishing, click "View reconciliation report" in the "You reconciled this account" window that appears.

11.7- Creating an Expense in QuickBooks Online

You can create an expense in QuickBooks Online to enter company expenses not entered into one of the other transaction expense forms, like the "Check" or "Bill" windows. For example, you can use the "Expense" window to record an in-store purchase.

To record an expense in QuickBooks Online:

1. Hover over the "+ Create" button in the Navigation Bar.
2. Select "Expense" under "Vendors."

Figure 117: A picture of the "Expense" window in QuickBooks Online. The numbers and letters match the steps in this activity.

3. Choose the payee from the drop-down menu.
4. Select the account from which to pay.
5. Enter the payment date.
6. Select the payment method.
7. Enter a reference number if needed.
8. Enter expense details:
    a. Use "Category details" for general expenses.
    b. Use "Item details" for products/services.
9. Add or delete rows as needed.
10. Type a memo if needed.
11. Attach files if needed.
12. Manage the expense using the toolbar:
    a. Click "Cancel" to cancel.
    b. Click "Clear" to clear the info.
    c. Click "Make Recurring" for regular expenses.
    d. Click "Save" to save.
    e. To save it and close the window or open a new window, click or select a choice from the “Save and new / Save and close” drop-down button.

13. After saving the expense, use the "More" button in the toolbar for additional options like copying, voiding, or deleting the expense, if needed.

11.8- Connecting Bank and Credit Card Accounts to QuickBooks Online

QuickBooks Online lets you connect to account feeds or upload account transaction files to import bank account and/or credit card account transactions into QuickBooks Online.

To connect bank accounts and credit card accounts to QuickBooks Online:

1. Select "Accounting" and then "Bank transactions" from the "All apps" bar to open the "Bank transactions" page.
2. If it's your first time, to connect a bank or credit card account:
   a. Use the "Search by name or sign-in URL" field to search for your bank, click it to select it, and follow the instructions.
3. If it's your first time, to import transactions:
   a. Click "Upload transactions" and follow the instructions.

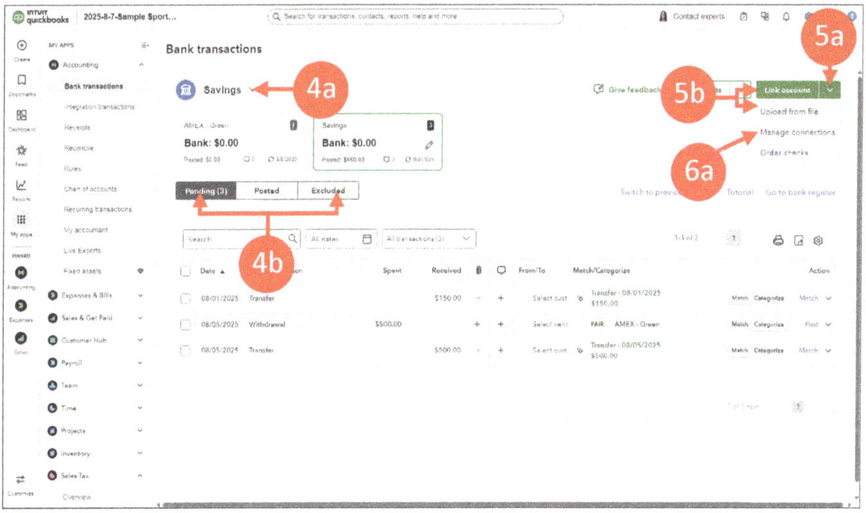

Figure 118: A picture of the "Bank transactions" page in QuickBooks Online after you connect an account or upload account transactions. The numbers and letters correspond to the steps in this activity.

4. To view transactions:
   a. Use the upper-left drop-down to select the account.
   b. Click the "Pending," "Posted," or "Excluded" tabs to see the selected account's transactions below the tabs.
5. To link a new account or upload transactions after the first time:
   a. Click the drop-down in the upper-right corner.

   b. Select "Link account" or "Upload from file."

6. To manage account connections:

   a. Use the "Manage connections" link in the drop-down.

11.9- Managing Connected Bank and Credit Card Account Transactions in QuickBooks Online

After you connect bank accounts and/or credit card accounts in QuickBooks Online, you can then review their pending transactions to either match them to existing transactions, categorize them and post them as new transactions, or exclude them from QuickBooks Online.

To manage connected bank and credit card account transactions in QuickBooks Online:

1. Select "Accounting" and then "Bank transactions" from the "All apps" bar to open the "Bank transactions" page.

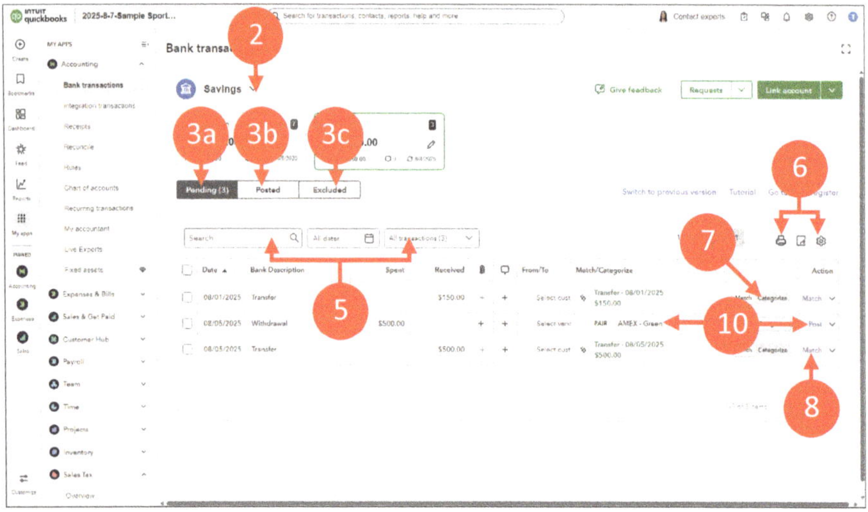

Figure 119: A picture of the "Bank transactions" page in QuickBooks Online. The numbers and letters match steps 2 through 10 in this activity.

2. Use the upper-left drop-down to select the account.
3. To see different types of transactions, click the tabs:
   a. "Pending" shows transactions to review.
   b. "Posted" shows matched and posted transactions.
   c. "Excluded" shows excluded transactions.
4. To review transactions, click “Pending.”
5. To filter the “Pending” transactions, use the “All dates” or “Status” drop-downs or type values into the “Search” field.
6. To print, export, or change the “Pending” tab’s settings, use the three buttons in the upper-right corner of the transactions list.

7. If needed, to switch between finding a matching QuickBooks transaction or categorizing a transaction, click its "Match/Categorize" toggle switch.
8. To match a recognized "Pending" transaction, click "Match" in its "Action" column to move it to the "Posted" tab.
9. To manually try to match an unmatched transaction, switch to its "Match" toggle option, check the checkbox for the matching transaction in the window that opens, and then click "Match."
    a. If matches aren't found, change the search and filter settings in this window to look for other possible matches or click the "Cancel" button in this window to close it if no matches exist.
10. To categorize a transaction and post it to QuickBooks Online, enter any missing details, use the "Match/Categorize" drop-down to select its account, and click "Post" in its "Action" column.

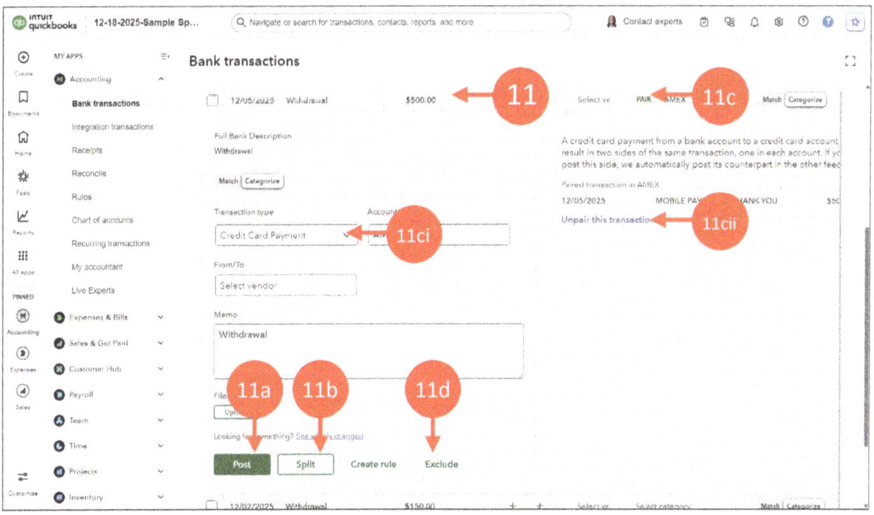

Figure 120: A picture of an expanded transaction in the "Bank transactions" page of QuickBooks Online. The numbers and letters match step 11.

11. If needed, to show additional transaction details when categorizing a transaction, click it to expand it and then edit its fields, as needed.
    a. To then post and add the transaction to the "Posted" tab, click "Post."

b. To split the transaction, click “Split,” split the amount to multiple accounts, then click “Split and post” to add it to the “Posted” tab.

c. QuickBooks adds a "Pair" tag to any "Pending" transaction it thinks may be paired to a transaction in another account to better match transfers and credit card payments. When posted, it posts both transactions.

   i. If needed, to change the transaction type, expand the record and use the "Transaction type" drop-down.

   ii. To unpair the transactions, click the "Unpair this transaction" link.

d. Alternatively, to exclude the transaction, if needed, click the “Exclude” button at the bottom of the expanded section to move it to the “Excluded” tab.

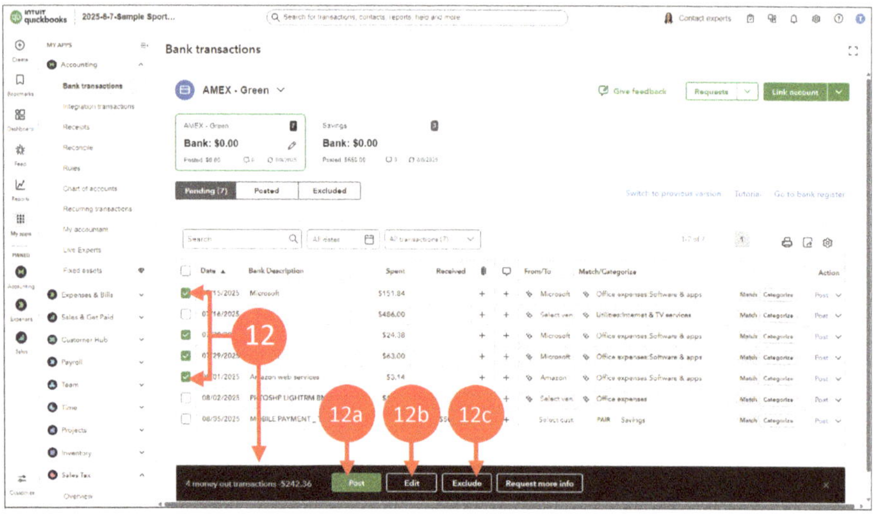

Figure 121: A picture showing multiple selected transactions in the "Bank transactions" page in QuickBooks Online. The numbers and letters match step 12 in this activity.

12. To post, edit, or exclude multiple “Pending” transactions as a batch action, check the checkboxes to select multiple transactions and show a new toolbar. In the toolbar:

    a. Click "Post" to post them.

    b. Click "Edit" to update, make changes, then “Apply” or “Apply and post.”

   c. Click "Exclude" to exclude.

13. To undo categorizing or excluding a transaction, find the transaction on the “Posted” or “Excluded” tab and click the "Undo" link in its "Action" column to move it back to "Pending."
14. To undo multiple “Posted” or “Excluded” tab transactions as a batch action, check the checkboxes to select multiple transactions and click “Undo” in the new batch action toolbar that appears.

CHAPTER 12- REPORTING

12.1- Running Reports in QuickBooks Online

QuickBooks contains many standard reports you can run to view information about your company. You can then customize and save these standard reports, as needed, to show the specific information you want.

To use standard reports in QuickBooks Online:

1. Click the "Standard reports" link in the "Reports & Analytics" bar.
2. Scroll through the reports at the right side of the page.

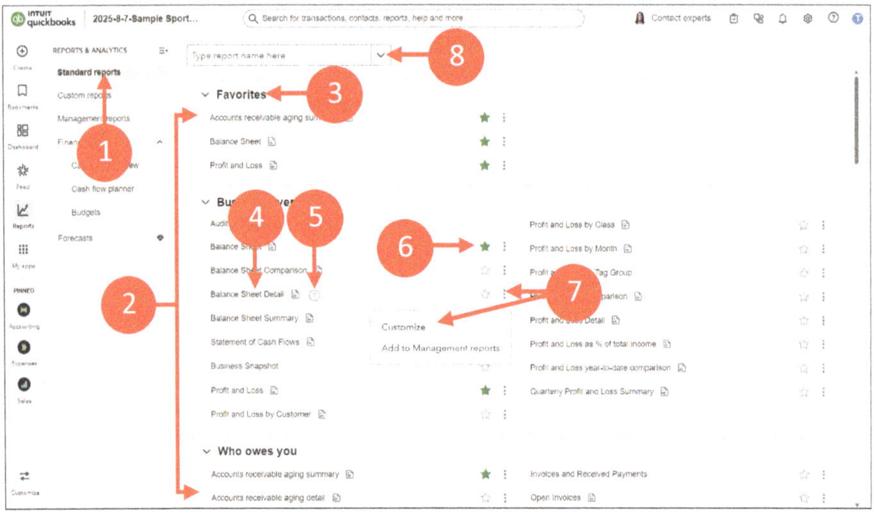

Figure 122: A picture of the "Standard reports" page in QuickBooks Online. The numbers match the steps in this activity.

3. Expand or collapse report categories by clicking their names.
4. Run a report by clicking its name.
5. See a report description by hovering over its name and clicking the question mark icon.
6. Add or remove a report from Favorites by clicking the star icon.
7. Customize a report by clicking the triple-dot icon and selecting "Customize."

8. Find a report by name by typing its name in the search field.

12.2- Customizing Reports in QuickBooks Online

QuickBooks Online lets you customize the standard reports it provides. You can then save these as custom reports you can quickly access in the "Custom reports" page. Older companies using QuickBooks Online may see reports in either a Classic view or a Modern view. New companies in QuickBooks Online only see the Modern view. The view slightly changes its customization options. Intuit is transitioning all reports to the Modern view.

To customize a standard report in QuickBooks Online:

1. Run the standard report you want to customize.
2. If needed and if available, to switch its view, click either "Switch to modern view" or "Switch to classic view" at the top of the report.

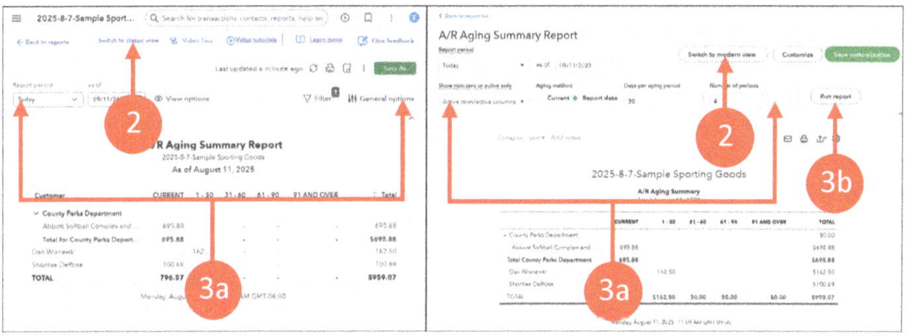

Figure 123: The left side of the picture shows a report in the Modern view, and the right side of the picture shows a report in the Classic view. The numbers and letters match the steps in this activity.

3. To customize a report:
    a. Change the options in the section above the report.
    b. Then click "Run report" to update if using classic view.

4. Classic view options in the toolbar directly at the top of the report:

Figure 124: A picture of a Profit and Loss report in its Classic view. The numbers and letters match the steps in this activity.

   a. To expand/collapse subaccounts, click the "Expand/Collapse" link.
   b. To sort, select a choice from the "Sort" drop-down.
   c. To add notes, click the "Add notes" link, type the notes at the bottom of the report, then click outside the notes to set them.

5. Modern view options:

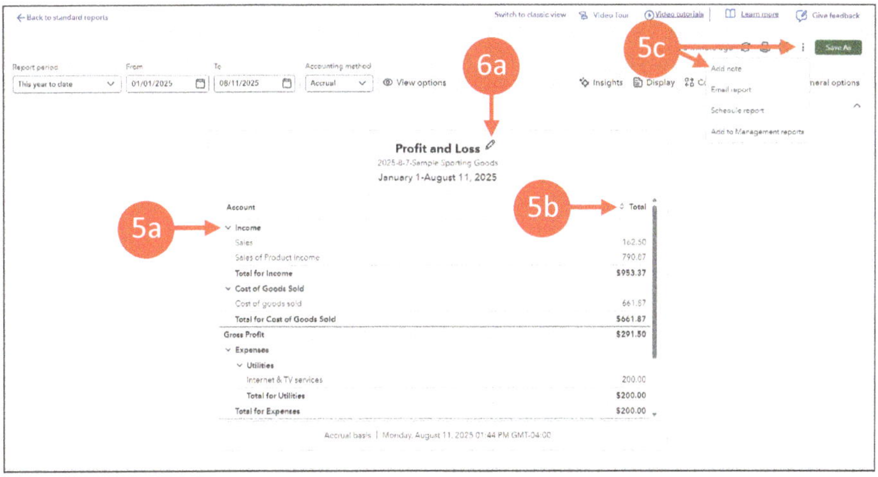

Figure 125: A picture showing the Profit and Loss report in the Modern view. The numbers and letters match the steps in this activity.

   a. All subaccounts appear expanded and to collapse them you must click the arrow next to the expanded account in the report.
   b. To sort, click the sort arrow button next to the column heading with the values by which to sort to show an "up" or "down" arrow for the sorting direction.
      i. To reverse the sort order, click its arrow again.
   c. To add notes, click the "More actions" drop-down, select "Add note," type notes at bottom of report, click outside the notes box.

6. To edit the report title in either view:
   a. Hover over the report's title, click the pencil icon that appears, then edit the title's text.
   b. To apply it, click into the blank area in the toolbar above the header if using the classic view or click outside the report title field if using the modern view.

7. To apply advanced report customization:
    a. In Classic view, click "Customize" at the top of the report to open the customization pane, make your changes, then click “Run report” in the pane.

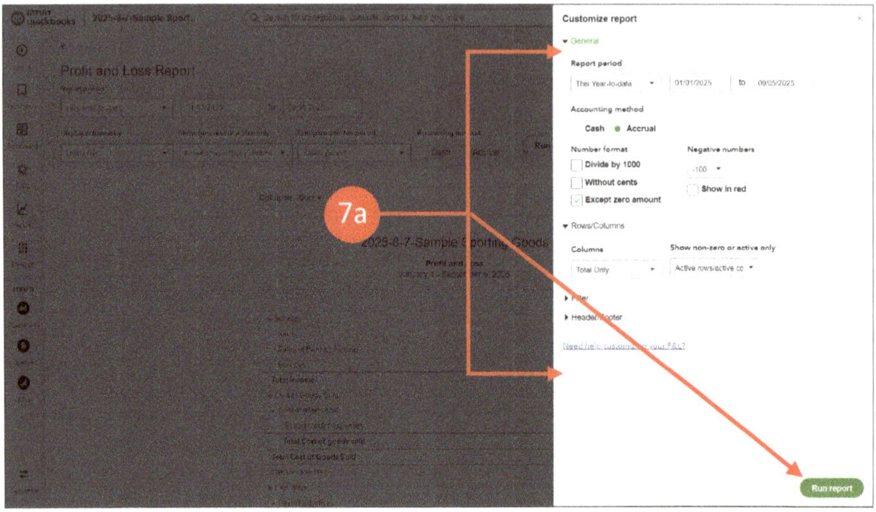

Figure 126: A picture of the "Customize report" pane for a Profit and Loss report in Classic view, showing where to click for this step in this activity.

    b. In Modern view, click the buttons at the right end of the report customization section to open their associated customization panes and make the changes in the pane.

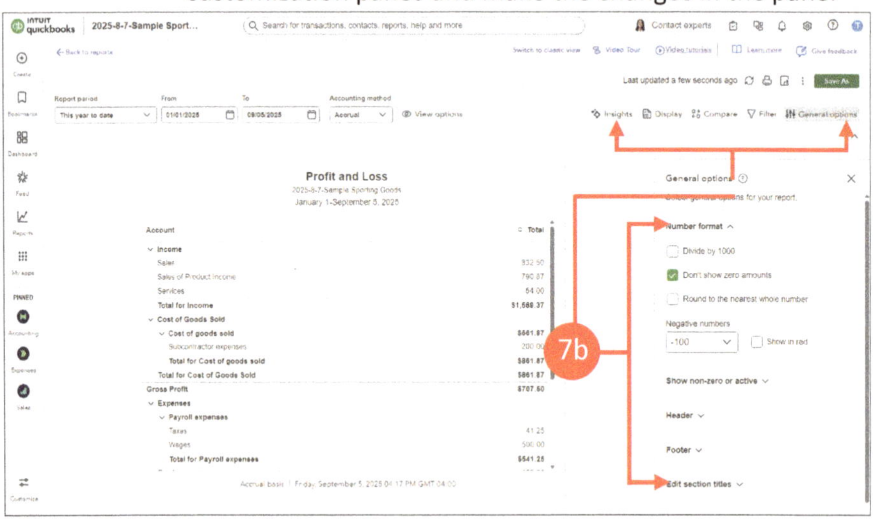

Figure 127: A picture of the report options for a Profit and Loss report in Modern view, showing where to click for this step in the activity.

12.3- Saving a Custom Report in QuickBooks Online

After customizing a standard report in QuickBooks Online, you can save it as a custom report, so you won't need to apply the customizations again. You access the custom reports in QuickBooks Online in the "Custom reports" page.

To save a standard report as a custom report in QuickBooks Online:

1. Open a standard report in QuickBooks Online and make the report customizations you want to save.
2. Click "Save customization" (Classic view) or "Save As" (Modern view).
3. Type a custom report name.
4. Click "Save."

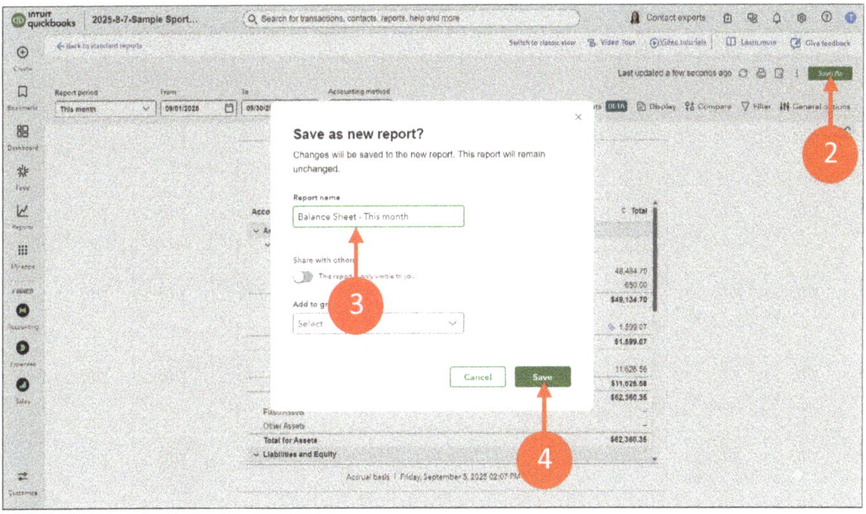

Figure 128: A picture showing how to save a custom report in QuickBooks Online. The numbers match the steps in the preceding activity.

To run a custom report in QuickBooks Online:

1. Click the "Custom reports" link in the "Reports & Analytics" bar.
2. Click the report name to run it.

12.4- How to QuickZoom Report Data

QuickZoom in QuickBooks Online lets you see details for report lines. Click any report line that looks like a link when you hover over it to then open either a new detail report or transaction for the referenced report line.

12.5- Creating Customer and Vendor Detail Reports

QuickReports were quick transaction detail reports you could create in QuickBooks Desktop Pro for customers, vendors, and accounts. While QuickBooks Online lacks the exact same capability, you can easily create these types of reports with some basic report customization in QuickBooks Online.

To create a customer or vendor detail report in QuickBooks Online:

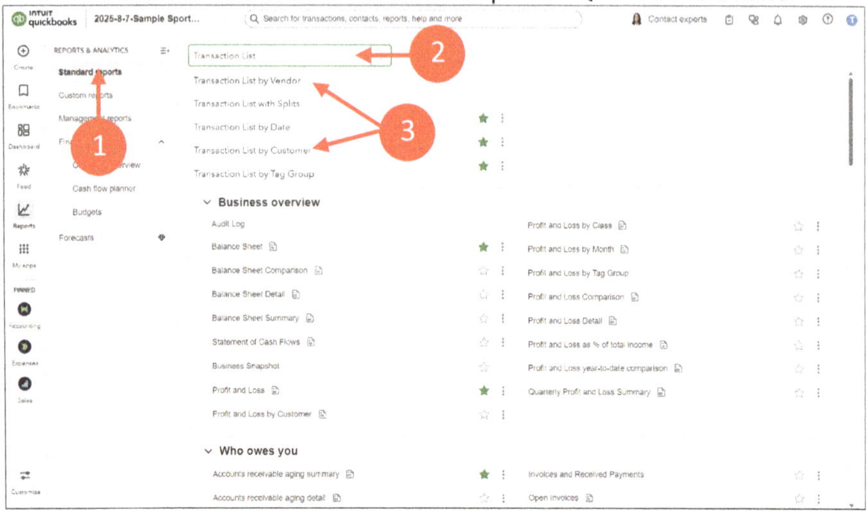

Figure 129: A picture showing how to run a customer or vendor transaction list report. The numbers match the steps in this activity.

1. Click the "Standard reports" link in the "Reports & Analytics" bar.
2. Type "Transaction List by Customer" or "Transaction List by Vendor" into the search bar.
3. Click the desired report's name in the search results.
4. To customize the report:

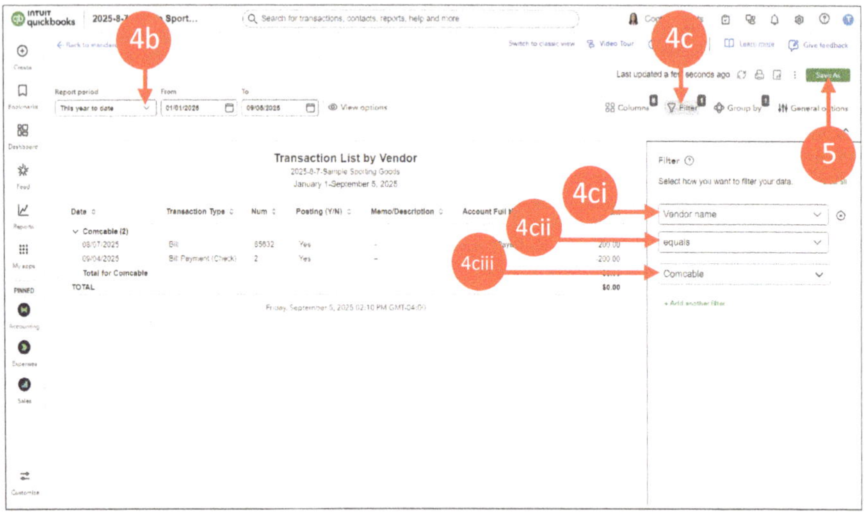

Figure 130: A picture showing how to customize a report to make a vendor detail report in QuickBooks Online. The numbers and letters match the steps in this activity.

   a. Click "Switch to modern view," if needed.
   b. Set the date range using the "Report period" drop-down.
   c. Click "Filter" to open the "Filter" pane.
      i. Select either "Vendor name" or "Customer name" from the top drop-down in the pane, as needed.
      ii. Select "equals" or "equals including sub-vendor/sub-customer" from the next drop-down.
      iii. Select the name of the desired vendor or customer from the final drop-down
5. To save the custom report, click the "Save As" button, type a new report name, and click "Save."

12.6- Creating an Account Detail Report

An account detail report in QuickBooks Online helpfully shows the transactions for an account in the Chart of Accounts.

To create an account detail report in QuickBooks Online:

1. Click the "Settings" button in the QuickBooks Online toolbar.
2. Select "Chart of accounts."
3. Find the desired account in the list.
4. Click or select "Run Report" in the account's "Action" column.
5. Change the date range using the "Report period" drop-down.
6. To save the custom report, click the "Save As" button, type a new report name, and click "Save."

12.7- How to Email, Print, and Export Reports

You can email, print, and export reports in QuickBooks Online to send them to others in the desired format.

To email, print, and export reports in QuickBooks Online:

1. Run the report in QuickBooks Online
2. If using Classic View:
   a. To email, print, or export a report as a PDF, click either "Email," "Print," or click "Export" and select "Export to PDF" to open a "Print, email, or save as PDF" window.
      i. Here, set the page orientation and check or uncheck the "Smart page breaks" (if available) and "Repeat page header" checkboxes, as desired.
      ii. To print the report, click the "Print" button in the toolbar at the top of the PDF preview to open a

"Print" dialog box, set the print settings, and print the report.

iii. To email the report, click the "Email" button in the "Print, email, or save as PDF" window.

1) In the "Email Report" window that opens, enter email addresses into the "To" and "CC" fields, edit the "Subject," "Body," and "Report" fields, if desired, and click the "Send" button.

iv. To save the report as a PDF, click the "Save as PDF" button in the "Print, email, or save as PDF" window to download the file as a PDF to your computer.

b. To download the report as an Excel workbook, click the "Export" button in the upper-right corner of the report after running it and then choose "Export to Excel."

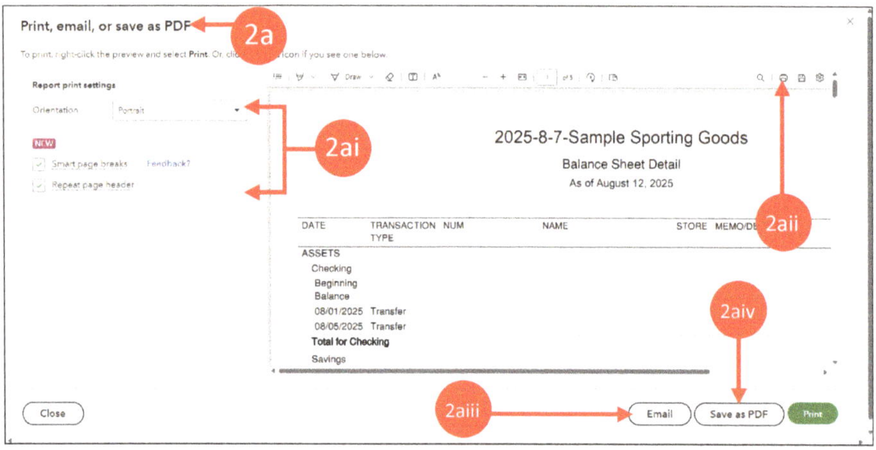

Figure 131: A picture of the "Print, email, or save PDF" window in QuickBooks Online. The numbers and letters match the steps in this activity.

3. If using Modern View:

a. To print or save a report as a PDF, either click the "Print" button in the report options section at the top of the report or click the "Export" button in this same area and select "Export to PDF" to open a "Print or save as PDF" window.

i. Here, set the page orientation and scaling using the drop-downs and check or uncheck the "Show report headers on all pages" checkbox, as desired.

ii. To print the report, click the "Print" button in the toolbar at the top of the PDF preview to open a "Print" dialog box, set the print settings, and print the report.

iii. To save the report as a PDF, click the "Save as PDF" button in the "Print or save as PDF" window to download it.

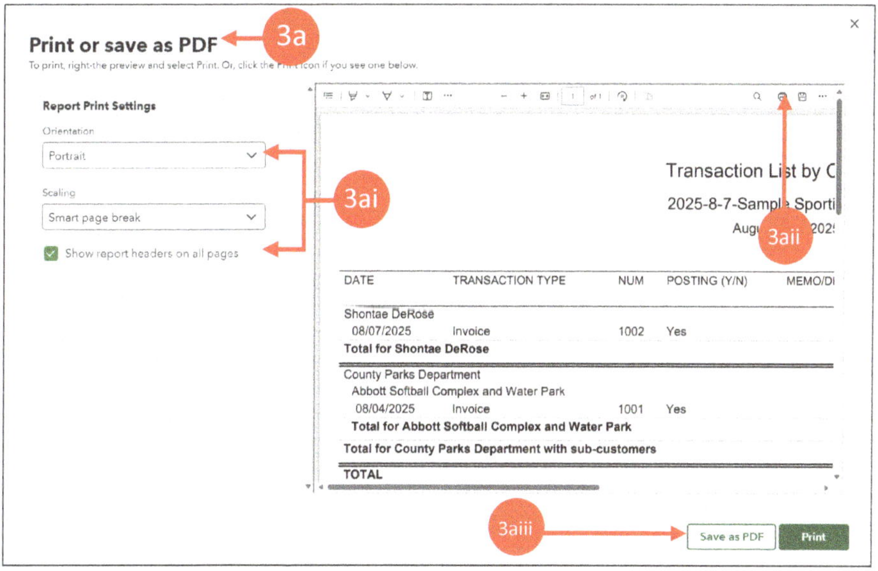

Figure 132: A picture of the "Print or save as PDF" window in QuickBooks Online. The numbers and letters match the steps in this activity.

b. To email a report as an Excel, CSV, or PDF attachment, click the "More actions" drop-down button in the upper-right area of the report, which looks like 3 vertical dots, and select "Email report" to open a "Send (Report Name) Report" window.

   i. Here, enter email addresses into the "To" and "CC" fields, edit the "Subject," "Message," and "FileName" fields, as desired, select a "Format" setting option to set the report's email attachment file format, and click "Send email."

c. To download the report to your computer as an Excel or CSV file, click the "Export" button in the report.
   i. To download the file as an Excel workbook, then select “Export to Excel.”
   ii. To instead download the file as a CSV, select “Export as CSV.”

CHAPTER 13- PROJECTS AND ESTIMATES

13.1- Creating a Project in QuickBooks Online

Projects in QuickBooks Online Plus or higher help you track money earned and spent on customer jobs. You can see all this info in one place and run reports for each project.

To view and create projects in QuickBooks Online:

1. Click the "Projects" link in the "Projects" app in the "All apps" bar.
2. To create a project:
    a. The first time: Click "Start a project."
    b. After that: Click "New Project" in the page's upper-right corner.
3. Enter the project's details:

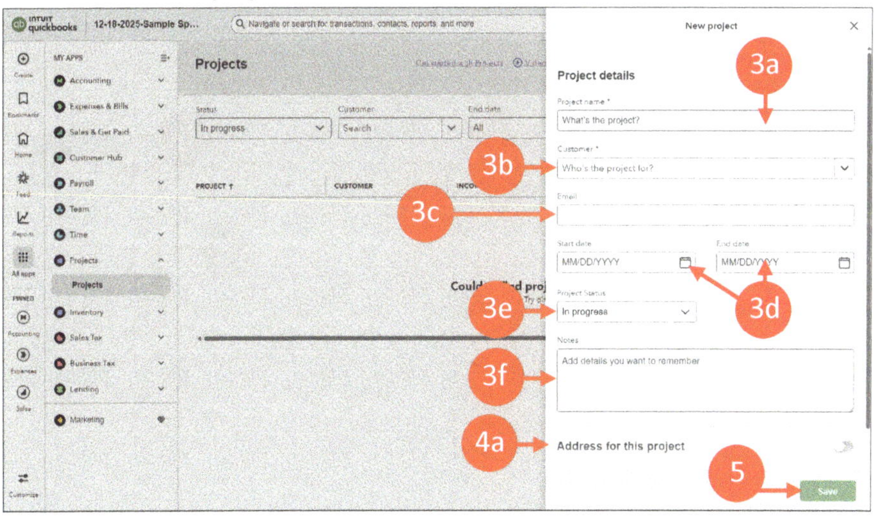

Figure 133: A picture of the "New project" pane in QuickBooks Online. The numbers and letters match the steps in this activity.

    a. Type the project's name in the "Project name" field.
    b. Choose the project's customer from the "Customer" drop-down.

   c. Enter the customer's email in the "Email" field if needed.
   d. Set start and end dates using the calendar drop-downs.
   e. Choose the project's status from the "Project Status" drop-down.
   f. Add notes or a description in the "Notes" field if you want.
4. To add project addresses:
   a. Turn on the "Address for this project" switch.
   b. Enter the customer's "Billing address" and "Shipping address" if needed.
5. Click "Save."

13.2- Adding a Transaction to a Project in QuickBooks Online

In QuickBooks Online Plus or higher, you can add transactions to a project to track income and expenses. You can add new transactions directly or classify existing ones. It's best to add estimates to the project before creating invoices from them. Also, add invoices to the project before receiving payments to avoid extra work.

To add a transaction to a project in QuickBooks Online:

1. To view projects in the “Projects” page, click the "Projects" link in the "Projects" app in the "All apps" bar.
2. Open the project's details page by clicking its entry in the "Projects" page.

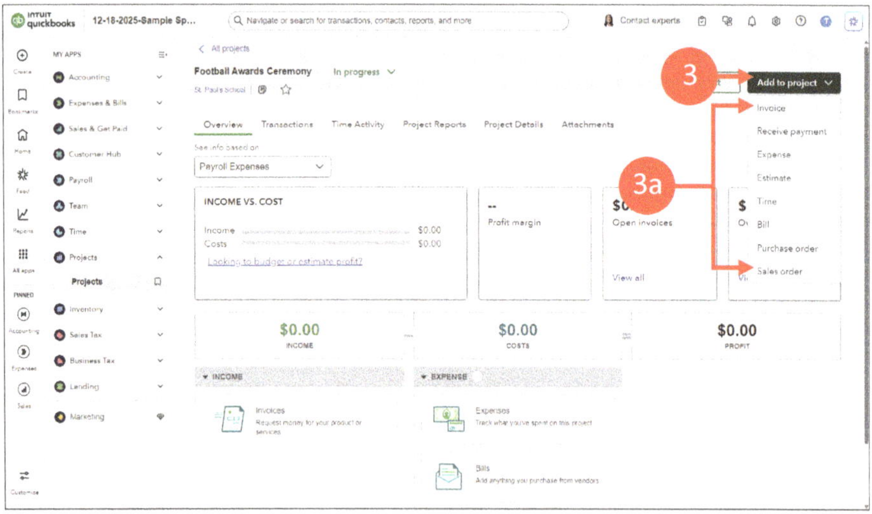

Figure 134: A picture showing how to add a transaction to a project. The numbers and letters match the steps in this activity.

3. Click the "Add to project" drop-down button in the upper-right corner.
    a. Select the type of transaction to add from the drop-down menu.
    b. Enter the transaction details.
    c. Ensure the "Customer" or "Customer/Project" field has the correct project info.
    d. Save the transaction.
4. To add an existing or new transaction to a project:

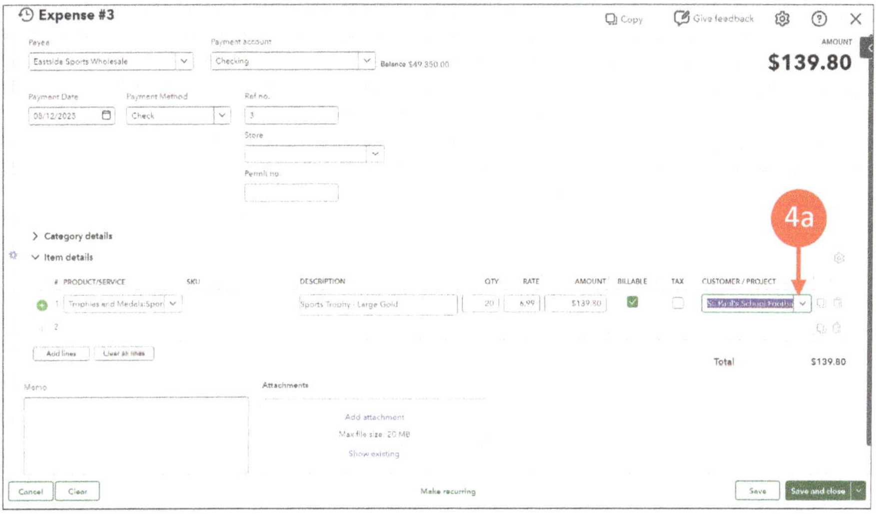

Figure 135: A picture showing where to assign a line item in an Expense to a project in QuickBooks Online. The number and letter matches the step in this activity.

    a. Select the project's name from the "Customer" or "Customer/Project" field when editing or entering the transaction's data.
    b. Save your changes.

13.3- Create an Estimate in QuickBooks Online

An estimate in QuickBooks Online is a quote for work you want to do for a customer. You can easily turn an estimate into an invoice without re-entering info. With progress invoicing, you can send partial invoices from the estimate. The estimate must be "Accepted" or "Pending," saved, and not fully invoiced to transfer its info to an invoice.

To create an estimate in QuickBooks Online:

1. To create an estimate from the Navigation Bar:
    a. Hover over the “+ Create” button in the Navigation Bar.

b. Click "Estimate" under the "Customer" heading.

2. Alternatively, to create an estimate from a project's details page:
    a. Click "Add to project" in the upper-right corner.
    b. Select "Estimate" from the drop-down.

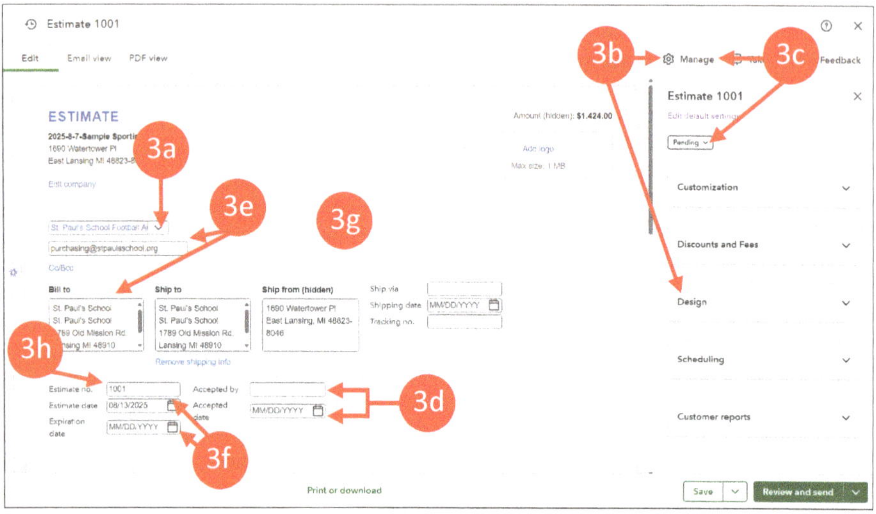

Figure 136: A picture of the top area of an estimate in QuickBooks Online. The numbers and letters match the steps in this activity.

3. Fill in the estimate's details:
    a. If needed, select the customer or project from the "Customer" drop-down.
    b. If needed, to change the estimate template, click "Manage" in the top toolbar then "Design" in the pane that opens, then select a template.
    c. If needed, to change the estimate's status, click "Manage" in the top toolbar, check the status at the top of the pane, and change it.
    d. In the estimate form, enter who accepted the estimate and the date, if needed.
    e. Edit the customer/project info at the top of the "Estimate" form if needed.
    f. Set the "Estimate date" and "Expiration date."
    g. Fill in shipping info, if enabled.
    h. Enter the estimate number if you turned on custom transaction numbers.

4. Add line items in the line items area:

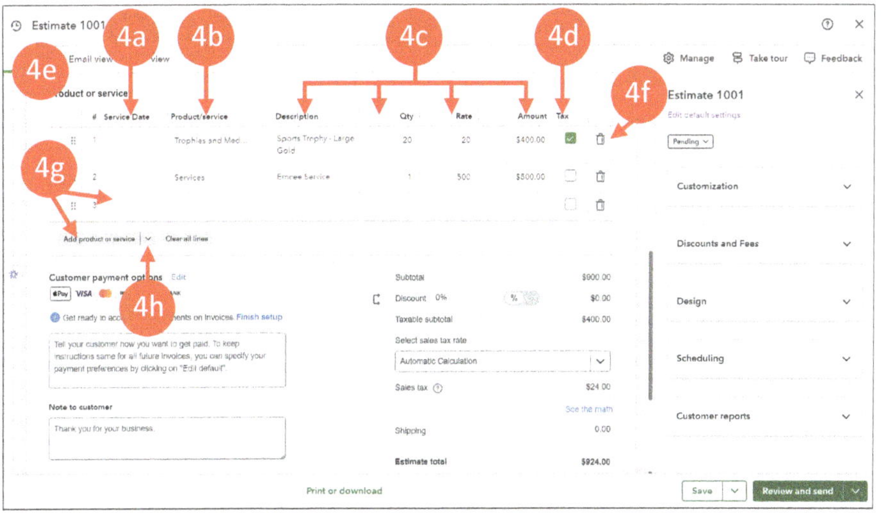

Figure 137: A picture of the line items area in an estimate. The numbers and letters match the steps in this activity.

   a. Select service dates, if needed.
   b. Choose items from the "Products & services" list.
   c. Enter their description, quantity, rate, and check the total line item amount, as needed.
   d. Check the "Tax" field if the item is taxable.
   e. Drag and drop to reorder line items.
   f. Delete line items by clicking the trash can icon button.
   g. Add new line items by clicking into the bottom row or clicking the "Add product or service" button.
   h. Add subtotal lines by selecting a row, clicking the drop-down on the "Add product or service" button, and then selecting "Add subtotal."

5. Add any optional notes or attachments:
   a. Enter a note to show on the estimate in the "Note to customer" field.
   b. Enter a statement message in the "Memo on statement" field.
   c. To attach files, drag and drop files onto the "Attachments" field or click it and use the "File Upload" dialog.

6. Check subtotal, sales tax, discount, shipping, and total fields.

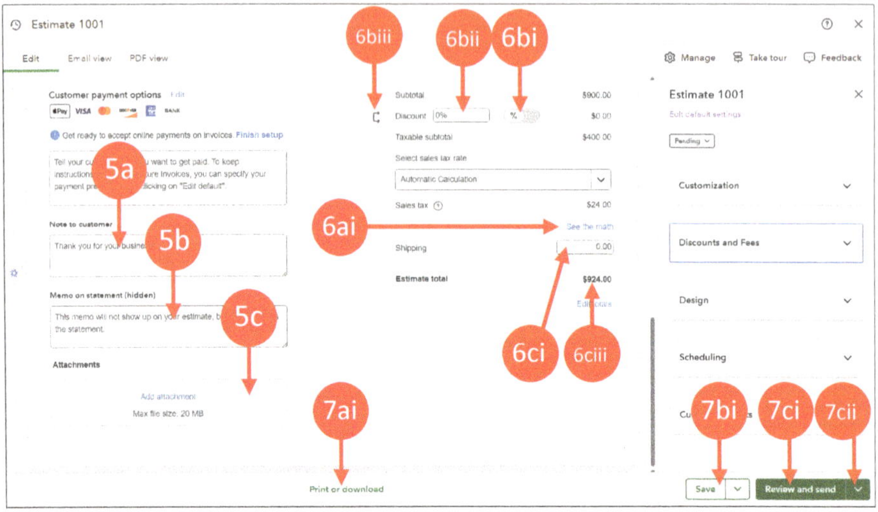

Figure 138: A picture showing the optional memo fields, the calculation fields, and the toolbar at the bottom of an estimate. The numbers and letters match the steps in this activity.

   a. To check sales tax:
      i. Click "See the math" by the sales tax amount to view and correct sales tax info.
      ii. To override the sales tax, click "Override this amount" in the pane that opens, then "Edit."
      iii. Enter a new "Rate" or "Amount" and select a "Reason for override."
      iv. Click "Apply override" and then "Close."
   b. To apply a discount:
      i. Click the "%" or "$" toggle switch.
      ii. Enter the discount percentage or amount.
      iii. Click the arrow buttons to change if the discount is applied before or after sales tax.
   c. To enter shipping:
      i. Enter the shipping amount in the "Shipping" field.
      ii. Check the tax on shipping, if needed.
      iii. The "Estimate total" field shows the total amount.
7. Save, print, or send the estimate:
   a. To print or download estimate:
      i. Click "Print or download" in the toolbar.

1) Select "Print" to open as a PDF and print or download.
2) Select "Download" to save a copy to your computer.

b. To save the estimate:

i. Click or select "Save," "Save and new," or "Save and close" from the drop-down button to save the estimate.

c. To send the estimate:

i. Click "Review and send" to save and send by text or email.

ii. Click the drop-down on "Review and send" and select "Share link" to email a link.

8. To perform actions on a saved estimate:

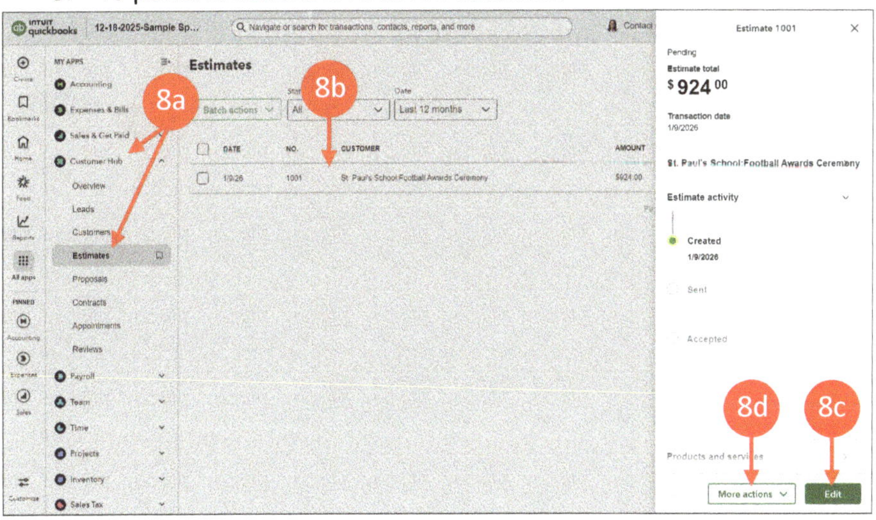

Figure 139: A picture showing the "Estimates" page and the pane that appears when you click an estimate in this page in QuickBooks Online. The numbers and letters match the steps in this activity.

a. Select the "Estimates" link under the "Customer Hub" app in the "All apps" bar to open the "Estimates" page.

b. Click the estimate in the "Estimates" page to see its info in a pane at the right side of the screen.

c. If desired, click "Edit" in this pane to reopen the estimate within the "Estimate" window.

i. To perform more actions within the reopened "Estimate" window, click "More actions" in its toolbar and then select actions like "Make a copy," "Delete," "Audit history," or "Copy to purchase order."

d. Alternatively, click "More actions" in this pane to select options like "Send," "Mark accepted," "Duplicate," or "Delete."

13.4- How to Duplicate an Estimate in QuickBooks Online

You can duplicate an existing estimate and then change the copy. This can save you time versus creating a new estimate from scratch. Duplicating an estimate helps if you have multiple customers who receive similar estimates for similar projects or if you need to create variations of an estimate for a project.

To duplicate an estimate in QuickBooks Online:

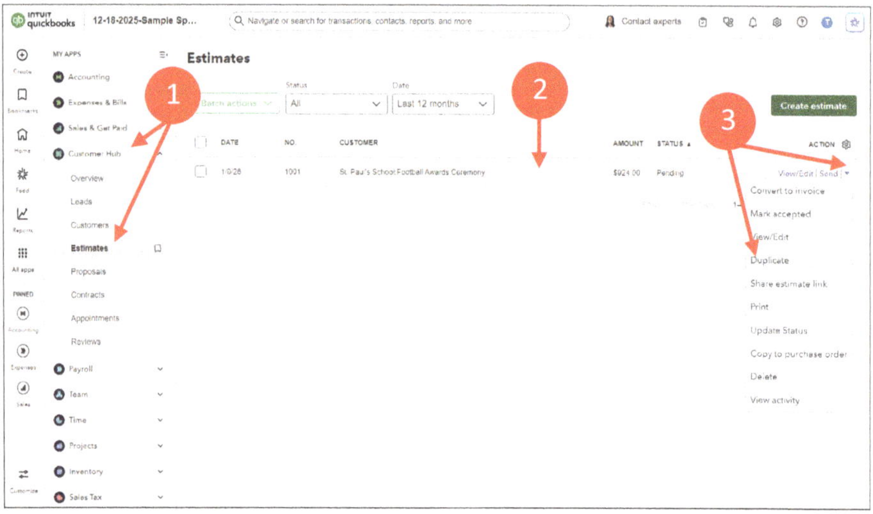

Figure 140: A picture showing how to duplicate an estimate. The numbers match the steps in this activity.

1. Select the "Estimates" link under the "Customer Hub" app in the "All apps" bar to open the "Estimates" page.
2. Locate the estimate to duplicate in the "Estimates" list.
3. Click the drop-down under its "Action" column and select "Duplicate" to open a new copy of the estimate.
4. The new estimate shows the next available estimate number.
5. Edit and save the copy of the estimate, as usual.

13.5- Invoicing from an Estimate in QuickBooks Online

Estimates let you easily turn them into invoices without re-entering info. With progress invoicing, you can send partial invoices from the estimate. The estimate must be "Accepted" or "Pending," saved, and not fully invoiced to transfer its info to an invoice.

If using QuickBooks Payments with estimates, customers can accept estimates in the forms you send, which changes their status.

Alternatively, to manually change an estimate's status in QuickBooks Online:

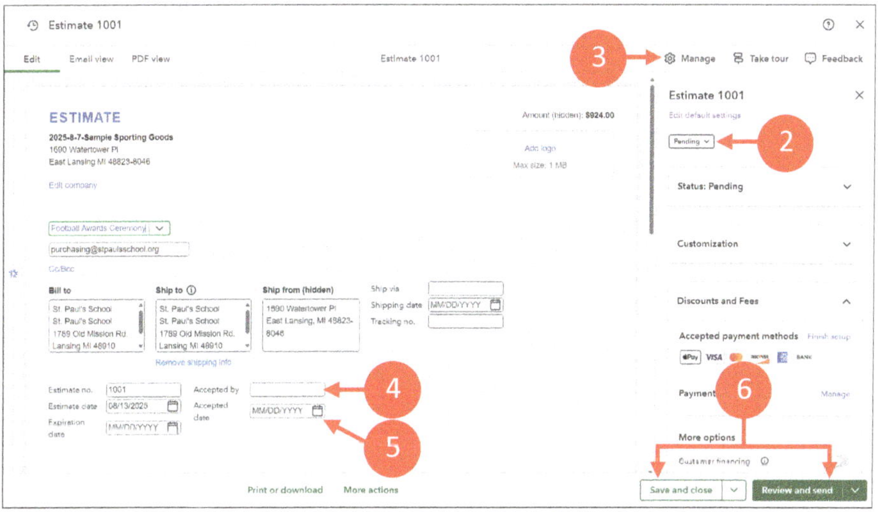

Figure 141: A picture of an estimate. The numbers match the steps in this activity.

1. Open the estimate.
2. Use the drop-down at the top of the pane on the right to change its status.
3. If you don't see the pane, click the "Manage" button in the toolbar.
4. In the Estimate form, enter who accepted the estimate in the "Accepted by" field.
5. Enter the acceptance date in the "Accepted date" field.
6. Save your changes.

Optionally, to enable progress invoicing in QuickBooks Online:

1. Click the "Settings" button in the QuickBooks Online toolbar.
2. Select "Account and settings" under the "Your Company" heading.
3. Click the "Sales" category on the left side of the “Account and settings” window.

4. Scroll down to the "Progress Invoicing" section at the right side of the window and click it to activate it.
5. Click to toggle the "Create multiple partial invoices from a single estimate" to the "On" position.
6. If needed, click the "Update" button in the confirmation window to update your invoice template.
7. Click the "Save" button at the bottom of the section.
8. Click the "Done" button to close the window.

Figure 142: A picture of the "Progress invoicing" setting in QuickBooks Online. The numbers match the steps in the preceding activity.

To invoice from an estimate in QuickBooks Online:

1. Select the "Estimates" link under the "Customer Hub" app in the "All apps" bar to open the "Estimates" page.
2. Find the estimate in the "Estimates" list and select the "Convert to invoice" command from the drop-down under its "Action" column.
3. If using full invoicing:
    a. The whole estimate converts to an invoice.
    b. Send the invoice as usual.
4. Alternatively, if using progress invoicing:
    a. A "How much do you want to invoice?" window opens.
    b. Then either:
        i. Select "Remaining total of all lines" for full amounts.

ii. Select "Percentage or amount" for partial amounts.

1) Enter the percentage or amount to invoice.

iii. Select "Manual entry for each line" for custom amounts.

c. Click "Create invoice."

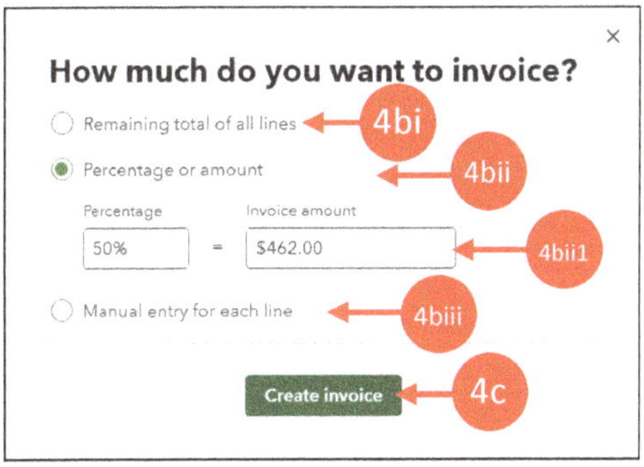

Figure 143: A picture of the progress invoicing options. The numbers and letters match the steps in this activity.

5. To enter line item amounts if you selected "Manual entry for each line":

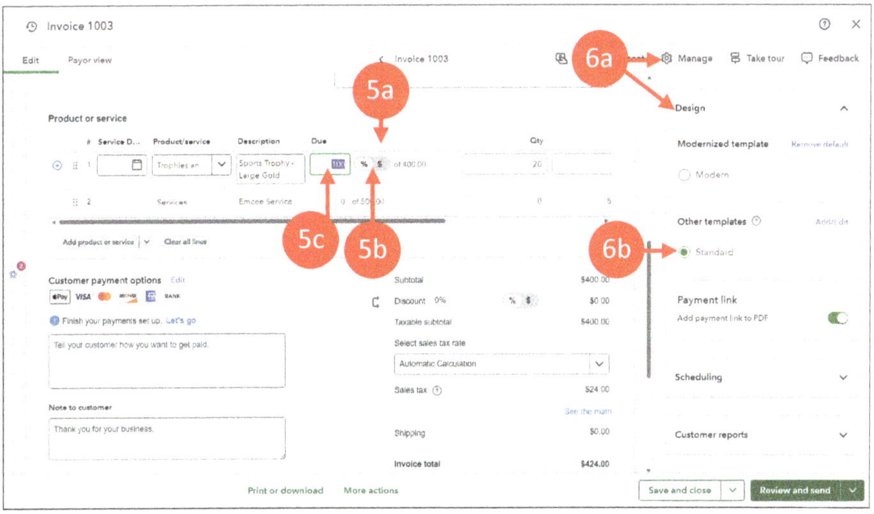

Figure 144: A picture showing manual entry for each line in a progress invoice. The numbers and letters match the steps in this activity.

a. Click into the "Due" column for each line item.

   b. Toggle "Percent/Amount" to choose which to enter.
   c. Enter the line item amount or percentage to bill.
6. If needed, to select the progress invoicing template:
   a. Click "Manage" in the top toolbar and click "Design" in the "Manage" pane.
   b. Select the progress invoice template.
7. Save and send the invoice, as usual.
8. If using progress invoicing, repeat this process for any remaining estimate amounts, as needed.

13.6- Invoicing for Billable Costs in QuickBooks Online

If you record costs for customers in QuickBooks and mark them as billable, like billable expenses or billable time, you can later invoice the customers for those billable costs.

To invoice for billable costs in QuickBooks Online:

1. Hover over the "+ Create" button in the Navigation Bar.
2. Click "Invoice" under the "Customers" heading to open a new "Invoice" window.

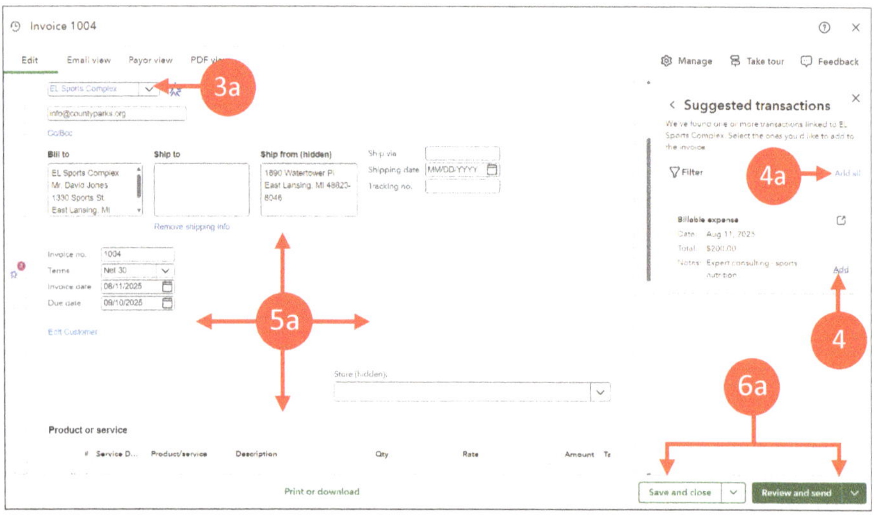

Figure 145: A picture showing how to add billable costs to an invoice. The numbers and letters match the steps in this activity.

3. Select the Customer or Project:
   a. Choose the customer or project from the "Customer" drop-down.
4. In the "Suggested transactions" pane, click "Add" next to the desired billable expense.

   a. Alternatively, to add all billable expenses and time, click "Add all."
5. Enter invoice information:
   a. Fill in any other needed invoice details.
6. Save the invoice:
   a. Click the desired "Save" button choice at the bottom of the window.

CHAPTER 14- PAYROLL

14.1- How to Run Payroll in QuickBooks Online

If you use a QuickBooks Online Payroll service, a setup wizard helps you enter all the needed info to create payroll. You can add employees and assign them to pay schedules as part of the setup. You can then pay the employees on a pay schedule.

To run a scheduled payroll in QuickBooks Online:

1. Select the "Payroll" app and then select the "Employees" link from the "All apps" bar.
2. Then click "Run payroll" in the upper-right corner of the "Employees" page.
3. Alternatively, hover over "+ Create" in the Navigation Bar and then click "Payroll" under the "Team" heading.
4. If needed, choose the pay schedule and click "Continue."

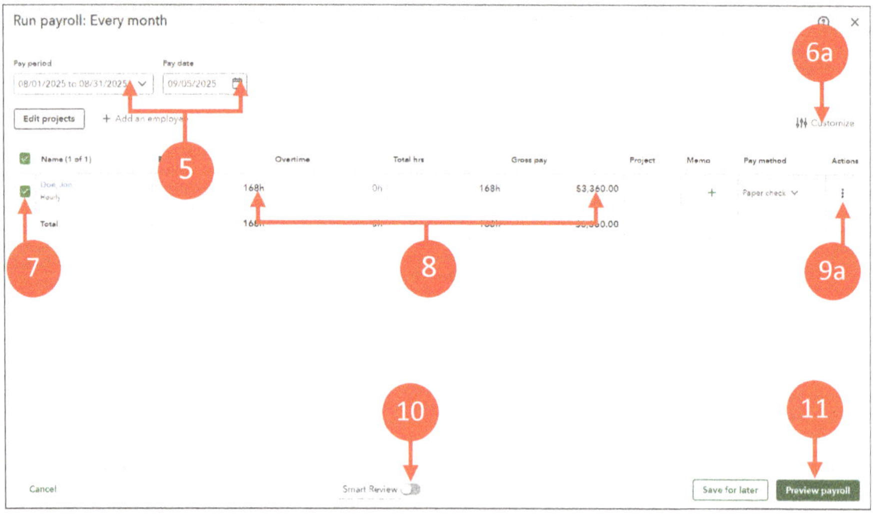

Figure 146: A picture of the first screen in the "Run payroll" window. The numbers and letters match the steps in this activity.

5. Check and change the "Pay period" and "Pay date," if needed.

6. Optionally, to customize the employees table:
    a. Click "Customize" to show or hide columns.
    b. Close the window by clicking "X."
7. Ensure the checkboxes for the employees to pay are checked.
8. Enter hours or pay amounts for each employee.
9. Optionally, to view and edit paycheck details:
    a. Click the triple-dot icon under "Actions" and select "Edit paycheck."
    b. Edit pay, taxes, and memo fields.
    c. Click "Save" to save changes or "Close" to exit.
10. Optionally, to turn Smart Review on or off, click the "Smart Review" toggle.
11. Click "Preview payroll."

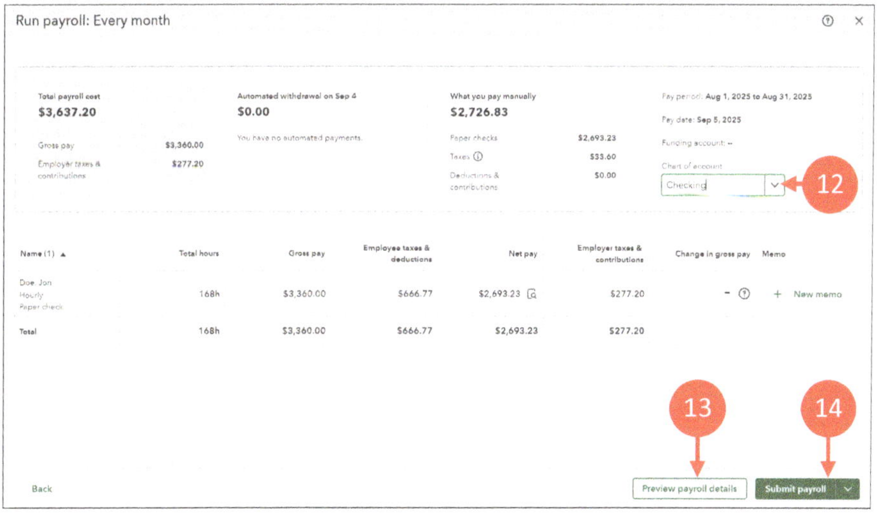

Figure 147: A picture of the second screen in the "Run payroll" window. The numbers and letters match the steps in this activity.

12. Select the account from which to withdraw the payroll from the "Chart of account" drop-down.
13. Click "Preview payroll details" to review the report.
14. To save or submit payroll, click or select a choice from the green drop-down button in the lower-right corner:
    a. Select "Save for later" to save changes and finish later.
    b. Click "Submit payroll" to finish and submit.

15. After you submit payroll, to print pay stubs or paychecks, click or select a choice from the "Print pay stubs/Print paychecks" drop-down button to open a PDF preview and print them.

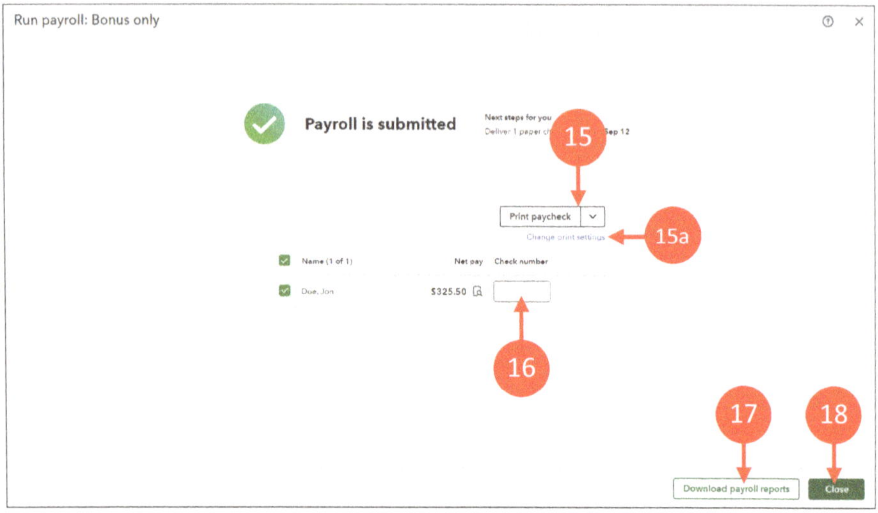

Figure 148: A picture of the final screen in the "Run payroll" window. The numbers and letters match the steps in this activity.

   a. To set up paycheck printing or change the print settings, click the link next to the drop-down button, change the settings, click "Save," then "Done."

16. If printing paychecks, you can also enter check numbers in the "Check Number" field.
17. To download payroll reports, click "Download payroll reports."
   a. Then check the reports to export and click "Export to Excel."
18. To close the Run Payroll window, click "Close" in its lower-right corner.

14.2- Printing, Editing, Deleting, and Voiding Paychecks

You might need to print, edit, delete, or void an employee's paycheck in QuickBooks Online. You can only edit the most recent paycheck if it hasn't been paid yet. For paper checks, the pay date must not have passed. For direct deposits, the check must not have been sent yet. If you can't edit a check, you might be able to delete or void it instead.

To print, edit, delete, or void a paycheck:

1. Select the "Payroll" app and then select the "Employees" link from the "All apps" bar.
2. Click the "Paycheck list" link in the upper-right corner.

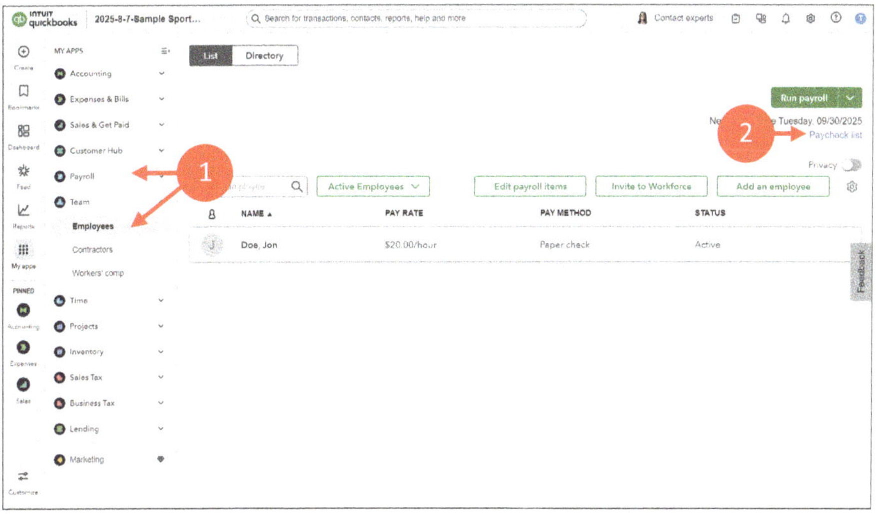

Figure 149: A picture of the "Employees" page in QuickBooks Online. The numbers match the steps in this activity.

3. To filter paychecks, click "Filter," select options, and click "Apply."
4. Click the paycheck's row to open its window.

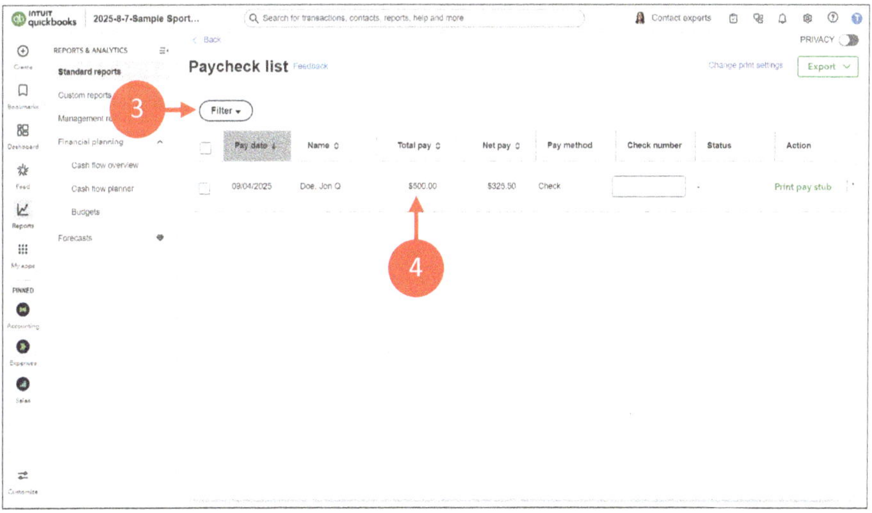

Figure 150: A picture of the "Paycheck list" window. The numbers match the steps in this activity.

5. To print the paycheck, click "Print" in the lower-right corner.

6. To edit, delete, or void the paycheck, click "Make adjustment" in the upper-right corner and choose the desired command.
7. If you are editing it, change its values, and click "Save" or "Close."
8. If deleting or voiding it, follow the prompts to finish.

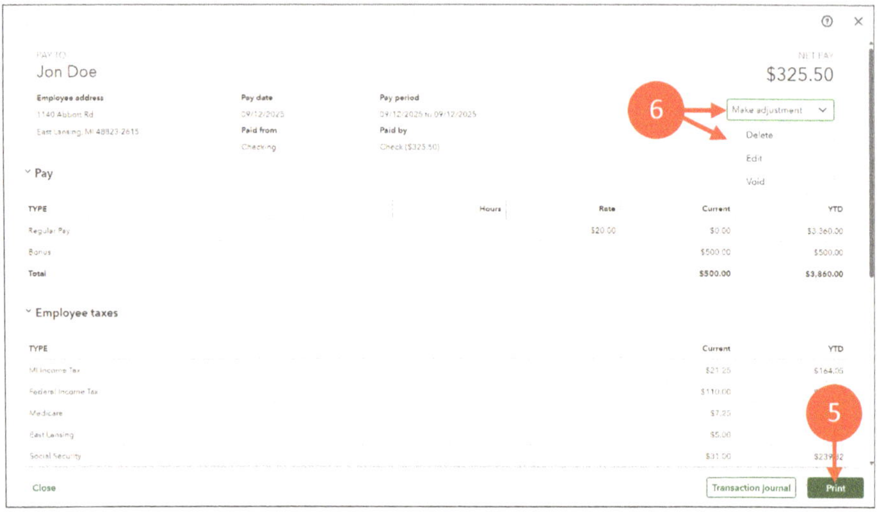

Figure 151: A picture of the paycheck details window in QuickBooks Online. The numbers match the steps in this activity.

To batch print pay stubs or paychecks or to reverse direct deposits:

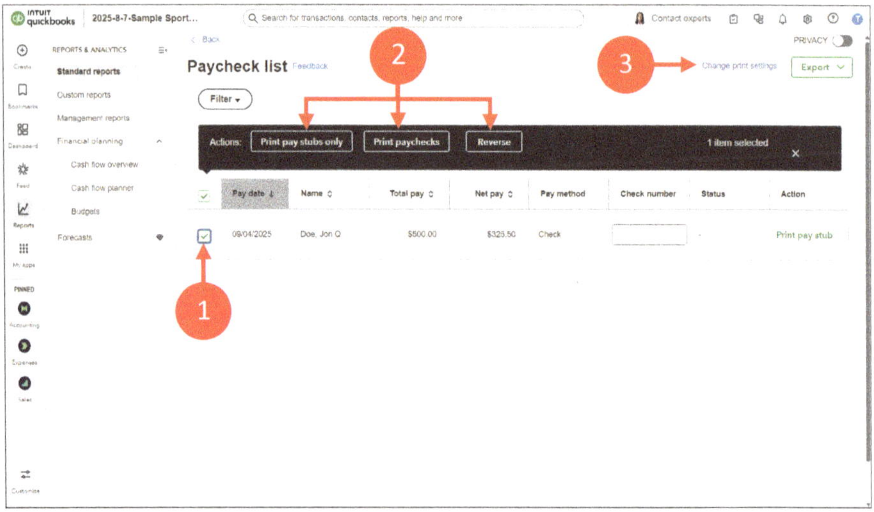

Figure 152: A picture of the "Paycheck list" window. The numbers match the steps in this activity.

1. Check the boxes next to the paychecks in the "Paycheck list" window.
2. Click the desired action button above the list.
3. If you can't see the "Print paychecks" button, then set up paycheck printing by clicking the "Set up paycheck printing" link and changing the "Print preferences."

TABLE OF FIGURES

INDEX

ABOUT THE AUTHOR

Joseph Brownell is founder and Vice President of TeachUcomp, Inc. He is the author of dozens of titles across the TeachUcomp, Inc. product line.